习英语的简单方法

LEI XIANGJIAN

版权所有。

版权所有©2018 由 Lei Xiangjian

未经出版商书面许可，不得以任何形式或通过电子或机械方式（包括影印、录制或任何信息存储和检索系统）复制或传播本书的任何部分。

此版本包含完整文本

原版精装版。

没有一个字被省略。

习英语的简单方法

一本令人发指的书 发表于

与作者的安排

BAD CREATIVE 出版历史

The Simplest Way To Learn French 2016年3月出版

The Simplest Way To Learn Spanish, 2017年3月出版

即将上市的作品

The Simplest Way To Learn Italian 2, 2019

ISBN-10: 1727207866   ISBN-13: 978-1727207866

Vol. 1

Vol. 2

ALSO AVAILABLE IN

- AUDIO
- HARDCOVER
- E-BOOK

FORMATS

SOCIAL #TheSimplestWay #LearnEnglish #BadCreativ3

内容

第1章 – **基础** _____ 1

第2章 – **餐饮** _____ 2

第3章 – 动物 _____ 3

第4章 – 所有格 _____ 4

第5章 – **服装** _____ 5

第6章 – 质询 _____ 6

第7章 – 动词 _____ 7

第8章 – **介词** _____ 8

第9章 – **日期和**时间_ 9

第10章 – **家庭** _____ 10

第11章 – 颜色 _____ 11

第12章 – 职业 _____ 12

第13章 – **措施** _____ 13

第14章 – **家庭** _____ 14

第15章 – **形容词** ___ 15

第16章 – **限定词** ___ 16

第17章 – **副词** _____ 17

第18章 – **物体** _____ 18

第19章 – **地点** _____ 19

第20章 – 人 _____ 20

第21章 – 编号 _____ 21

联系方式 Contact

前言

在学校里，我们学到了一些今天可能没有用的东西。 然而，语言是至关重要的人类状况的几乎每一个方面。

你如何拓展你的业务超出你的大陆更多的销售？ 你打算如何表达你对刚刚走过的美丽女士的爱？ 如何从希思罗机场到达酒店？ 随着语言的知识，这就是如何。

本书包含日常英语会话中一些最常用单词的词典。 它利用重复和死记硬背的古老学习技巧，尽快调节大脑学习英语。 此外，还包括一个称为故事模式的辅助功能，以帮助读者进行理解测试。最后，应该指出的是，虽然这本书将有助于视觉识别和英语单词的理解，但学生也必须了解他们正确的发音。 为了帮助这一点，有一个伴随的有声读物，将提供，使听力课程。

所以，从美丽的城市伦敦，城市的红色巴士和所有的东西时尚，我们为您介绍简单的方法来学习英语。

如何使用本书

1. 这条线是训练线（如果你愿意，可以是T线）

训练时间

它代表了一套二十五个字要记住的结束。

2. **您需要覆盖**书的右侧并尝试翻译左侧。
3. **每个正确的翻译都有1分。**在T线之后但不高达25的**任何东西都被视为奖金。**
4. **在得分至少达到20分之前，不要进入下一批**
5. **故事模式旨在帮助您理解句子中单词的用法，因此请务必在培训中获得高分，以便充分理解故事。**

既然你知道规则，

让我们开始吧。

第1章

基础

关键词：I, a, he, she, you, and, the, guy, girl, man, woman, apple, eat, drink, water.

の	The
水	Water
林檎	Apple
男の子	Boy
女の子	Girl
おとこ	Man
女性	A woman
パン	Bread
男	A man
女性	A woman
私は男です	I am a man
私は男の子です	I am a boy
女性がリンゴを食べる	The woman eats an apple
その少年はリンゴを食べる	The boy eats an apple
彼女はいる	She is
彼は男の子です	He is a boy
彼女は女の子です	She is a girl
私は飲む	I drink
あなたが飲む	You drink
私は食べる	I eat
あなたが食べる	You eat
彼女は食べる	She eats
砂糖を食べる	I eat sugar
彼は水を飲んでいます	He is drinking water
あなたは女性です	You are a woman

训练时间

女性たち	Women
その本	The book
新聞	Newspaper
私は読む	I read
私は書きます	I write
あなたが読む	You read
あなたが書く	You write
彼女は読む	She reads
彼が読みました	He read
私たちは書く	We write
我々は飲む	We drink
彼は本を書いた	He wrote a book
あなたは水を飲む	You drink water
私たちは水を飲みます	We drink water
彼女は飲んでいます	She is drinking
彼は水を飲んでいます	He is drinking water
あなたは男の子です	You are a boy
私たちは子供です	We are children
私たちは男性です	We are men
私たちは女性です	We are women
私たちは男の子です	We are boys
あなたは男です	You are a man
牛乳を飲むのですか？	Do we drink milk?
牛乳を飲む	We drink milk
私たちは水を飲みます	We drink water

训练时间

後期	The
午後に	they
こんにちは！	We, they
中国語	Late
私は言った	In the afternoon
どうもありがとうございました	Hello there!
さようなら	Chinese
あなたは英語を話せますか？	I said
私はJamesで、英語を話します	Thank you very much
はい、ご容赦ください	Goodbye
私は黄です、私はイタリア語を話すことができます	Can you speak English?
それはリンゴですか？	I am James and I speak English
彼、彼女、私たち	Yes, please forgive me
彼らは男性ですか？	I'm Huang, I can speak Italian
彼らは女性ですか？	Is it an apple?
彼らは男性だ	He, she, we
彼女たちは女性です。	Are they men?
彼らは女の子です	Are they women?
彼らが読んで	They are men
彼らは書きます	They are women.
彼女たちは女性です。	They are girls
後期	They read
午後に	They write
こんにちは！	They are women.

训练时间

谢谢	Thank you
是	Yes
你好	Hello there
再见！	Goodbye!
晚上好	Good evening
早上好	Good morning
晚安	Good night
再见	Goodbye
再见萨尔瓦多	Goodbye Salvador
格鲁吉亚晚上好	Good evening Georgia
晚安乔	Goodnight Joe
谢谢索非亚！	Thank you Sofia!
不，谢谢	No, thank you
不抱歉	No sorry
请	Please
对不起	I am sorry
在糖	In sugar
我有一个苹果	I have an apple
我吃了糖	I ate sugar
这个男孩写道	The boy wrote
她吃糖	She eats sugar
我有一本书	I have a book
他在喝啤酒	He is drinking beer
我喜欢你	I like you
我喜欢女人	I like women

训练时间

我们是女人	We are women
他们是女孩	They are girls
我有一把钥匙	I have a key
他们不好	They are not good
他们读	They read
他们喜欢菠萝	They like pineapples
男孩吃一个苹果	The boy eats an apple
这个人读了这封信	This person read this letter
我读了这些文字	I read these texts
女孩正在吃一个苹果	The girl is eating an apple
他读了这些话	He read these words
她正在写作	She is writing
她吃土豆	She eats potatoes
他们喜欢香蕉	They like bananas
她是非常好的	She is very good
他们喝	They drink
你们都是女孩	You are all girls
我写了一本书	I wrote a book
你写了一封信	You wrote a letter
我写	I write
他写了一本书	He wrote a book
那男孩写了一封信	The boy wrote a letter
我读了报纸	I read the newspaper
他们读了一本书	They read a book
他们写了一本书	They wrote a book

训练时间

我们读	We read
我们喝	We drink
我独自一人	I am alone
你读了一本书	You read a book
我们看报纸	We read the newspaper
他阅读一本书	He reads a book
丹妮是一个人	Zhao is a person
玛蒂娜写道，翔吉读了它	Huang wrote that, Xiang Ji read it
阿尔贝托读一本书	Alberto reads a book
早上好你好吗？	Good morning, how are you?
我是一个女孩，我喝牛奶	I am a girl and I drink milk
你喝水	You drink water
我为什么这么说？	Why do I say that?
我们不想要一个敌人	We don't want an enemy
她问道并回答	She asked and answered
谁赢？	Who wins?
我必须六点起床	I must get up at six
这是一个承诺	This is a promise
我把水装满了瓶子	I filled the bottle with water
我们这样做	We do this
我做的	I did it
我听说	I heard
我非常喜欢他们	I like them very much
她帮助他们	She helps them
我的兄弟找他们	My brother looks for them

训练时间

故事模式

ENGLISH

Zhu: "I'm ready to party with the players in Rio de Janeiro. We're leaving tomorrow."

Huang: "Do you have everything you need?"

Zhu: "Yes."

Huang: "How long is your trip?"

Zhu: "About three to four months."

Huang: "What is in this bag?"

Zhu: "Not much, some clothes, water and computers."

Huang: "Have you considered the necessary things for your arrival?"

Zhu: "What do you mean?"

Huang: "A place to live, places to eat, places to go."

Zhu: "No, not really."

Huang: "If you haven't booked a place yet, you can still stay at the Wharf Palace Hotel. Breakfast is very cheap and includes fresh milk.

For food and drinks, you can visit Acqua, a very nice place in Sao Paulo. They also have a garden where you can sit and drink with men and women

In the evening, you should go to 'Cambery' beach. There is always a group of happy people looking for a good time.

Finally, if you want to buy items, you can visit Ordem Market. It is open on Saturday, but most traders speak Portuguese."

Zhu: "No problem, I can read a little Portuguese. I can also learn the language when I arrive."

Huang: "Will your sister go with you?"

Zhu: "Yes, we will write a book together."

Huang: "What about your father?"

Zhu: "No, he will be able to read newspapers at home."

Huang: "Well, don't forget about us and bring back some souvenirs."

Zhu: "Don't worry, I'll send letters to update you."

Huang: "Thank you, I will be very grateful."

A B C D E F G H I
J K L M N O P Q
R S T U V W X Y
Z

CHINESE

朱："我已经准备好与里约热内卢的球员进行派对，我们明天就要离开了。"

黄："你有你需要的一切吗？"

朱："是的。"

黄："多长时间就是你的旅行吗？"

朱："大概三到四个月。"

黄："什么是在这个袋子吗？"

朱："不多，有些衣服，水和电脑。"

黄："你有没有考虑必要的东西为您的到来？"

朱："你是什么意思?"

黄："一个住的地方，地方吃饭，要去的地方"

朱："不，不是真的。"

黄："如果你还没有订了一个地方，你仍然可以留在码头宫酒店。早餐是非常便宜，包括新鲜牛奶。

对于食品和饮料，你可以访问Acqua，一个非常不错的地方在圣保罗。 他们还有一个花园里，你可以坐下来喝与男子和妇女

在晚上，你应该去'坎伯里'海滩。 总是有一个集团的快乐的人在寻找一个好的时间。

最后，如果您想购买的物品，可以访问的Ordem市场。 它是开放的，上周六，但是，大多数交易商讲葡萄牙语"

朱："没问题，我可以读一点葡萄牙语，我也可以学习语言，当我抵达。"

黄："将你的妹妹跟你一起去吗？"

朱："是的，我们将编写一本书在一起。"

黄："什么有关你父亲的吗？"

朱："没有，他将可以在家里，读报纸。"

黄："好吧，不要忘了我们，并且还带回了一些纪念品。"

朱："不要担心，我会送你的字母，让你更新。"

黄："谢谢你，我将非常感激。"

1 2 3 4 5 6 7 8 9 10 11 12 13 14 15 16 17 18 19 20 21 22 23 24 25 26 27 28 29 30 31

第2章

餐饮

关键词： Chocolate, fruit, carrot, food, beer, bottle, coffee, breakfast, cut, eat, cook.

水果	Fruit
叉子	Fork
饥饿	Hunger
饮食	Diet
早餐	Breakfast
午餐	Lunch
晚餐	Dinner
瓶子	Bottle
玻璃	Glass
黄油	Butter
杯子	Cup
这个碗	The bowl
蛋糕	Cake
啤酒	Beer
鸡	Chicken
鸡蛋	The egg
一个鸡蛋	An egg
饮料	Beverage
奶酪	Cheese
一个红萝卜	A carrot
酱	Sauce
葡萄	Grape
大蒜	Garlic
果汁	Juice
饮料	Drink

训练时间

鱼	Fish
牛奶	Milk
咖啡	Coffee
菜单	Menu
这餐	The meal
碟子	Plate
一根香蕉	A banana
我吃巧克力	I eat chocolate
男孩吃饼干	The boy eats cookies
我吃巧克力冰淇淋	I eat chocolate ice cream
我吃午饭	I am having lunch
我做午餐	I make lunch
它不酸	It is not sour
果酱具有酸味	The jam has a sour taste
我煮肉	I cook meat
这是一个厨房	This is a kitchen
我喝了一瓶	I drank a bottle
你喝牛奶	You drink milk
你喝咖啡	You drink coffee
你吃鱼	You eat fish
这个人有叉子	This person has a fork
我吃炸奶酪	I eat fried cheese
我们吃	We eat
我们吃早餐	We have breakfast
厨师有黄油	The chef has butter

训练时间

女人是吃鱼	The woman eats fish
我吃晚饭	I have dinner
鱼是晚餐	The fish is for dinner
我不吃奶酪	I do not eat cheese
他们吃鱼	They eat fish
厨师切牛肉	The chef cuts beef
我砍苹果	I cut the apple
她做饭	She cooks
我煮鱼	I cook fish
女人切胡萝卜	The woman cuts carrots
我煮鸡肉	I cook chicken
奶油沸腾	The cream is boiling
巧克力奶油沸腾	The chocolate cream is boiling
菠萝和啤酒	Pineapple and beer
我剪了面包	I cut the bread
食物	The food
糖果	The candy
我吃水果	I eat fruit
他吃豆子	He eats beans
柠檬	Lemon
橙色	Orange
她吃了一根香蕉	She ate a banana
我吃了一块甜蛋糕	I ate a sweet cake
我吃牛排	I eat steak
他们吃果酱	They eat jam

训练时间

这肉	The meat
猪肉	Pork
洋葱	Onion
盐	Salt
糖	Sugar
汤	Soup
意大利面	Spaghetti
白饭	White rice
餐厅	Restaurant
三明治	Sandwich
番茄	Tomato
土豆	Potato
我煮土豆	I boiled potatoes
我吃了果酱	I ate jam
男人喝柠檬水	The man drinks lemonade
厨师煮猪肉	The chef cooks pork
我在书中有一个配方	I have a recipe in the book
她喝油	She drinks oil
我不喝油	I do not drink oil
我没有胡椒	I do not have pepper
我们吃意大利面	We eat pasta
我煮土豆	I boiled potatoes
这是一个三明治	This is a sandwich
他吃沙拉	He eats salad
厨师有个香肠	The cook has a sausage

训练时间

厨房	Kitchen
牛肉	Beef
葡萄酒	Wine
果汁	Fruit juice
烧烤	Barbecue
草莓	Strawberry
成分是盐	The ingredient is salt
我们在餐厅吃晚餐	We had dinner in the restaurant
这是一只火鸡	This is a turkey
女士们在餐厅吃午饭	The ladies have lunch at the restaurant
这个男孩吃午餐	The boy has lunch
女人吃晚饭	The woman eats dinner
我吃了一个番茄	I ate a tomato
厨师吃午餐	The chef has lunch
我不是服务员	I am not a waiter
我们喝果汁	We drink fruit juice
他剪了面包	He cut the bread
他阅读菜单	He reads the menu
他吃香蕉	He eats bananas
你饿了吗？	Are you hungry?
你喜欢胡萝卜吗？	Do you like carrots?
我做饭，你吃	I cook and you eat
我吃了一个鸡蛋	I ate an egg
他不是素食主义者	He is not vegetarian
厨师烹饪蘑菇	The chef cooks mushrooms

训练时间

刀	Knife
勺子	Spoon
苦	Bitter
一个柠檬	A lemon
农场	Farm
他吃蔬菜	He eats vegetables
服务员有酒	The waiter has wine
我们吃蘑菇	We eat mushrooms
我吃鱼	I eat fish
我不吃奶酪	I do not eat cheese
女孩是喝茶	The girl is drinking tea
女孩是饿了	The girl is hungry
成分是果酱	The ingredient is jam
味道不甜	The taste is not sweet
味道很甜	The taste is sweet
你吃冰	You eat ice
男孩吃奶酪	The boy eats cheese
我喜欢蛋糕	I like cake
我喜欢色拉与石油	I like salad and oil
我们吃一个菠萝	We eat a pineapple
我们吃一个苹果	We eat an apple
你喝咖啡吗?	Do you drink coffee?
他有水	He has water
他有一个苹果	He has an apple
他吃了一块饼干	He ate a piece of biscuit

训练时间

女孩吃水果	The girl eats fruit
女孩用胡椒粉吃意大利面	The girl eats pasta with pepper
女人喜欢用胡椒面食	The woman enjoys pepper pasta
你吃土豆吗?	Do you eat potatoes?
这个女孩喝橙汁	The girl is drinking orange juice
女孩们吃米饭	The girls eat rice
男人喜欢米饭与胡椒	Men like rice and pepper
我有一本书	I have a book
我喜欢巧克力	I like chocolate
他喜欢用胡椒做巧克力	He likes to make chocolate with pepper
我喜欢饼干	I like cookies
他喜欢喝茶	He likes to drink tea
我们吃三明治	We eat sandwiches
牛奶是沸腾的	Milk is boiling
食物很好	Food is good
他喝柠檬水	He drinks lemonade
这是一顿饭	This is a meal
这是食物!	This is food!
我不喝酒	I do not drink
他高兴地写道	He wrote happily
葡萄酒很好	Very good wine
我吃糖	I eat sugar
我做成酸奶	I make yogurt
你吃草莓吗?	Do you eat strawberries?
我喜欢牛排	I like steak

训练时间

不，弗朗西斯卡不吃鱼	No, Francesca does not eat fish
维多利亚吃米饭	Victoria eats rice
牛奶，鸡蛋，鱼	Milk, eggs, fish
我煮鱼	I cook fish
橙子是一种水果	Orange is a kind of fruit
丹妮吃水果	Zhao eats fruit
不，Han不喝酒	No, Han doesn't drink
这是一个番茄	This is a tomato
我吃意大利面	I eat pasta
我煮意大利面	I cook pasta
是的，它是果汁	Yes, it is juice
女孩们吃水果	Girls eat fruit
我们喝果汁	We drink fruit juice
是的，一个西红柿	Yes, a tomato
橘子，苹果	Orange, apple
我不煮面条，我煮米饭	I do not cook noodles, I cook rice
女孩吃草莓	The girl eats strawberries
不，它不是草莓，是番茄	No, it is not a strawberry, it is a tomato
李不吃草莓	Li does not eat strawberries
阿尔贝托不吃酱油	Alberto does not eat soy sauce
茶，水，糖	Tea, water, sugar
我吃三明治	I eat sandwiches
我们吃草莓	We eat strawberries
这是一个三明治	This is a sandwich
你吃三明治	You eat a sandwich

训练时间

不，汉是不是吃素	No, Han is not a vegetarian
草莓，苹果，水果	Strawberry, apple, fruit
男孩吃草莓	The boy eats strawberries
是的，一张是素食主义者	Yes, Zhang is vegetarian
素食主义者喝啤酒吗？	Do vegetarians drink beer?
张是一个素食主义者，她不吃鱼	Zhang is a vegetarian, she does not eat fish
我素食，我不吃鸡肉	I'm vegetarian, I don't eat chicken
它是汤	It is a soup
它是一个柠檬	It is a lemon
它是食品	It is food
番茄，土豆，奶酪	Tomato, potato, cheese
我煮鱼	I cook fish
番茄，洋葱，汤	Tomato, onion, soup
鸡蛋，奶酪	Eggs, cheese
我煮肉	I cook meat
午餐	Lunch
我吃午饭	I am having lunch
我吃肉	I eat meat
鱼，肉，鸡肉	Fish, meat, chicken
鸡蛋，鸡肉，大米	Eggs, chicken, rice
我不想吃生菜	I don't want to eat lettuce
我们的葡萄	Our grapes
一个胡萝卜和一个苹果	One carrot and one apple
汤是为赵	The soup is for Zhao
我不想在我的沙拉生菜	I do not want lettuce in my salad

训练时间

胡萝卜	Carrot
菠萝	Pineapple
不，他们不是葡萄	No, they are not grapes
是的，蘑菇是红色的	Yes, mushrooms are red
她喝水或牛奶	She drinks water or milk
沙拉，蘑菇，胡萝卜	Salad, mushroom, carrot
阿尔贝托吃蘑菇	Alberto eats mushrooms
西尔维娅和黄是素食者	Silvia and Huang are vegetarians
丹妮和我吃肉	Zhao and I eat meat
马可和我不喝啤酒	Marco and I do not drink beer
我想要沙拉里的蘑菇	I want a mushroom in a salad
是的，它是沙拉	Yes, it is a salad
我们吃菠萝	We eat pineapples
我想要的葡萄是红色的	The grapes I want are red
她吃了一根香蕉蛋糕	She ate a banana cake
你需要更多的玉米吗？	Do you need more corn?
我喝的时候我想	I drink when I want to
如果我不做饭，我不吃	If I don't cook, I don't eat
我想要一根香蕉	I want a banana
白蛋糕是我的	White cake is mine
它是菠萝吗？	Is it pineapple?
我想要更多香蕉	I want more bananas
我吃，因为你吃	I eat because you eat
酱，番茄，洋葱	Sauce, tomato, onion

训练时间

冰淇淋	Ice cream
我有咖啡冰淇淋	I have coffee ice cream
这顿饭	The meal
豆	Beans
蘑菇	Mushroom
菠萝是我们的	The pineapple is ours
她正在吃香蕉	She is eating a banana
我想要沙拉里的金枪鱼	I want tuna in the salad
土耳其不是我们的	The turkey is not ours
你需要更多的冰块吗?	Do you need more ice cubes?
我不吃意大利面	I do not eat pasta
我在晚餐时发言	I speak at dinner
金枪鱼,肉和鸡肉	Tuna, meat and chicken
我不想要土耳其,谢谢	I do not want turkey, thank you
我在吃东西时看了菜单	I read the menu when I was eating
这是冰,而不是糖	This is ice, not sugar
黄油和油	Butter and oil
油和盐	Oil and salt
你吃胡椒吗?	Do you eat pepper?
我想要没有奶酪的意大利面	I want pasta without cheese
我不吃大蒜	I do not eat garlic
即使她不喝啤酒,她也会喝	Even if she does not drink beer, she will drink
小明吃芝士饭	Xiaoming eats rice with cheese
油是黄色的	Oil is yellow
生菜	Lettuce

训练时间

故事模式

ENGLISH

Zhu: "What do we have for breakfast?"

Huang: "Carrot cake."

Zhu: "Is it a salad?"

Huang: "No, this is a real cake. It is made of carrots."

Zhu: "It looks delicious. I want to eat a cake made of bananas, oranges, strawberries or pineapple... how about lunch?"

Huang: "Rice and tuna, garlic sauce."

Zhu: "No, I don't want that. What else do you have in the fridge?"

Huang: "Nothing but some tomatoes, fish, chicken, cheese, onions and some eggs. I still need to buy some items."

CHINESE

朱:"我们早餐吃什么?"

黄:"胡萝卜蛋糕。"

朱:"它是一个沙拉?"

黄:"不,这是一个真正的蛋糕,它是用胡萝卜制成的。"

朱:"看起来很美味,我想吃一块用香蕉,橘子,草莓或者菠萝做的蛋糕……午餐怎么样?"

黄:"大米和金枪鱼蘸蒜酱。"

朱:"不,我不想那样。你在冰箱里还有其他什么食物?"

黄:"没有什么,只是一些西红柿,鱼,鸡肉,奶酪,洋葱和一些鸡蛋,我还需要购买一些物品"

第3章

动物

关键词： Whale, elephant, wolf, cow, insect, cat, snake, duck, shark, fly, ant, animal.

公牛	Bull
那匹马	Horse
那只鸟	Bird
乌龟	Tortoise
狮子	Lion
狗	Dog
那只猫	Cat
大象	Elephant
鸭子	Duck
蜘蛛	Spider
熊	Bear
那只兔子	Rabbit
猪	Pig
猴子	Monkey
海豚	Dolphin
一头牛	A cow
一只蜜蜂	A bee
一个昆虫	An insect
鲸鱼	Whale
她有一只猫	She has a cat
这是一只狼	This is a wolf
这是一只企鹅	This is a penguin
猴子在动物园里	A monkey in the zoo
你是一只老虎	You are a tiger
鸡是一只鸟	The chicken is a bird

训练时间

狗喝水	The dog drinks water
牛喝牛奶	The cows drink milk
猫饮用水	A cat drinks water
猫喝牛奶	The cat drinks milk
大象喝牛奶	Elephants drink milk
鸟儿吃水果	The birds eat the fruit
猴子吃一个香蕉	A monkey eats a banana
牛喝水	The cows drink water
蜘蛛饮用水	A spider drinks water
我是一只蝴蝶	I'm a butterfly
我是一只昆虫	I'm an insect
蛇吃老鼠	Snakes eat rats
鲨鱼吃	Sharks eat
该飞是在玻璃	The fly is in the glass
我有一只蜜蜂	I have a bee
我有一只熊	I have a bear
蜜蜂吃糖	The bees eat the sugar
狗吃蚂蚁	The dog eats ants
他们不喜欢马匹	They don't like horses
这是一只老鼠！	This is a mouse!
大象吃一个苹果	The elephant eats an apple
这个女孩说话的老虎	The girl talks to the tiger
狼会谈到的女孩	The wolf talks to the girl
蛇告诉这孩子说话	The snake told the child to speak
老虎吃面包	Tigers eat bread

训练时间

苍蝇吃面包	The fly eats bread
蚂蚁读一本书	The ant reads a book
这个动物	The animal
猫喝牛奶	The cats drink milk
马喝水	The horse drinks water
鸟儿喝水	The bird drinks water
马是一种动物	A horse is an animal
狼喝牛奶	The wolf drinks milk
是的，狗	Yes, the dogs
我喜欢猫	I like cats
昆虫吃巧克力	Insects eat chocolate
苍蝇吃巧克力	Flies eat chocolate
昆虫喝水	Insects drink water
苍蝇是昆虫	Flies are insects
他们是猫吗？	Are they cats?
这是一只蚂蚁	It is an ant
是的，他们是大象	Yes, they are elephants
胡安是一只乌龟	Juan is a turtle
阿尔贝托是一只鸭子	Alberto is a duck
费尔南多是一头大象	Fernando is an elephant
大象喝水	The elephants drink water
我们是乌龟	We are turtles
他们是螃蟹，而不是蜘蛛	They are crabs, not spiders
熊是一种动物	A bear is an animal
那些鸟儿	The birds

训练时间

故事模式

ENGLISH

Zhu: "Thank you for taking me to the zoo, there are so many animals here, I can see lions, horses, elephants, monkeys, bears, rabbits and birds."

Huang: "Look there, that giant spider is called the tarantula, and in the water, there are big turtles, ducks, crabs and dolphins."

Zhu: "Are there also penguins?"

Huang: "I doubt it, the penguin is an Arctic animal, so it's more likely to be in the frozen regions."

Zhu: "You know a lot about animals, do you have a pet?"

Huang: "No more. Once I had a mouse, and then a pig, but my sister ate it. Then there was a dog that loved to chase the neighbor's cat, but it got sick and died."

Zhu: "Which animals are your favorites?"

Huang: "The animals I like best are the ones I can eat or drink, especially chickens and cows. The ones I hate the most are snakes and bees."

CHINESE

朱："谢谢你带我去动物园，这里有很多动物，我可以看到狮子，马，大象，猴子，熊，兔子和鸟类。"

黄："看那里，那只巨型蜘蛛被称为狼蛛，水里有大乌龟，鸭子，螃蟹和海豚。"

朱："还有企鹅吗？"

黄："我对此表示怀疑，企鹅是一种北极动物，所以它更可能在冰冻地区。"

朱："你对动物有很多了解，你有宠物吗？"

黄："没有更多。 有一次，我有一只老鼠，然后是一只猪，但我的妹妹吃了它。 然后有一只狗喜欢追逐邻居的猫，但它生病并死亡。"

朱："哪些动物是你最喜欢的？"

黄："我最喜欢的动物是我可以吃或喝的，尤其是鸡和牛。 我最讨厌的是蛇和蜜蜂。"

第4章

所有格

关键词：My, yours, hers, mine, ours, mine.

这不是我的。	It's not mine.
我吃我的三明治。	I eat my sandwich.
我的猫喝的牛奶。	My cat drinks milk.
这些狗是我的。	These dogs are mine.
这狗是我的。	This dog is mine.
我的苹果是板上。	My apple is on the plate.
她是我的女朋友。	She's my girlfriend.
这个猫不是我的。	This cat is not mine.
这是你的吗？	Is it yours?
我们喝你的。	We'll drink yours.
你的三明治。	Your sandwich.
厨房是你的。	The kitchen is yours.
他有你的板。	He's got your plate.
还有一碗在你的厨房。	There's a bowl in your kitchen.
我吃你的。	I'm eating yours.
你的盐。	Your salt.
叉子是你的。	The fork is yours.
我会吃你的三明治。	I'll eat your sandwich.
她的意大利面是一盘。	Her pasta is on a plate.
糖果是她的。	The candy is hers.
他的马吃饭	His horse eats rice
我有他的瓶子。	I have his bottle.
这是她的叉子。	It's her fork.
你的蝴蝶。	Your butterfly.
石油是他的。	The oil is his.

训练时间

动物吃它的食物	The animal eats its food
这是我们的	This is ours
我们写在我们的菜单	We write in our menu
我们的面食在盘子里	Our pasta is on the plate
马不是我们的	The horse is not ours
蜜蜂是我们的	The bees are ours
猫是我们的	The cat is ours
他的猫吃老鼠	His cat eats mice
我有我们的母牛	I have our cow
她吃自己的糖果	She eats her own candy
你的刀不切	Your knife does not cut
我们的猫不喝水	Our cat does not drink water
他有自己的猫	He has his own cat
女人有你的眼镜	The woman has your glasses
我们吃我们的蛋糕	We eat our cake
我没有你的瓶子	I don't have your bottle
动物吃自己的食物	The animals eat their own food
这个男孩吃他自己的饼干	The boy is eating his own cookies
你的鸭子喝水	Your duck drinks water
你的动物吃更多的肉	Your animal eats more meat
我爸喝了酒	My dad drinks wine
苹果是我们的	The apple is ours
是的，这些钱是我的	Yes, this money is mine
我想要我的面包	I want my bread

训练时间

故事模式

ENGLISH

"This dress is like mine." the lady said.
"Most clothes have similar nuances in our shop… Look, this is a red ribbon and yours is blue." The gentleman replied.
"Look at that man for example. He also bought something similar for his daughter, but it has a pocket."
"You are right, I understand." said the woman.

CHINESE

"这件衣服是类似于我的,小姐说场的。"
"**大多数的衣服在我们的商店也有类似的细微差别…你看,这是一个红色丝带和你的是蓝色的,先生回答说。**"
"看看那个男人为例子,他也购买了类似的东西为他的女儿但是它有一个口袋里。"
"你是对的,我明白了。"这位女士说的。"

第5章

服装

关键词： Uniform, jewelry, clothes, sweater, dress, clothing, shoe, trousers, bag, belt, gloves, shirts, boots, socks, pockets, jacket, sandal.

裤子	Pants
领带	Tie
皮带	Belt
服装	Clothing
裙子	Skirt
衬衫	Shirt
鞋子	Shoes
衣服	Clothes
手袋	Handbags
帽子	Hat
凉鞋	Sandals
帽子是紫色的	The hat is purple
礼服	The dress
口袋	Pocket
我的鞋子	My shoes
她的裤子	Her pants
他有我的外套	He has my coat
我的衬衫	My shirt
我的夹克是棕色的	My jacket is brown
我有你的腰带	I have your belt
我的裤子	My pants
我有一条裙子	I have a skirt
我有衬衫	I have a shirt
我有你的鞋子	I have your shoes
刀是在鞋	The knife is in the shoe

训练时间

大衣	Coat
外套	Jacket
开机	Boot
均匀	Uniform
放养	Stocking
一件毛衣	A sweater
西装	Suit
我有一把雨伞	I have an umbrella
钱包是我们的	The wallet is ours
我有我的钱包	I have my wallet
我有珠宝	I have jewelry
她买靴子	She buys boots
蓝色的鞋子	Blue shoes
我的凉鞋	My sandals
手套是你的	The gloves are yours
男人有一个皮钱包	The man has a leather wallet
这是一个凉鞋	This is a sandal
他的袜子	His socks
这是一条裙子	This is a skirt
她的裙子是红色的	Her skirt is red
我们的衬衫	Our shirt
你需要一条白色的裙子	You need a white skirt
这件衣服是他的	This dress is his
这本书是黑色的	This book is black
他吃红肉	He eats red meat

训练时间

故事模式

ENGLISH

Huang: "Those shoes are very beautiful, they seem expensive."

Zhu: "Yes, I needed new clothes, so today I went shopping."

Huang: "Fantastic! what else did you buy?"

Zhu: "First, I bought a new dress for work and the yellow belt I was looking for last summer. Then I bought pants, a white dress, a coat for my mother and a pair of shirts for my father. As I left, I saw the boots under a pair of skirts, and decided to get them for you, along with a sweater."

Huang: "Thank you very much, I appreciate it."

"Today is very windy." Miss Alessia said as they left the mall.

"This is a sign that summer is ending." Laurent answered.

"I wish I had a jacket and a pair of socks."

"I think I have some socks in my bag." Mr. Laurent said.

"Do not worry, I can buy one in that other clothing store, I can see some good glasses for sale at the window!"

CHINESE

黄:"那双鞋很漂亮,看起来很贵。"

朱:"是的,我最近得到了支付,所以我去了购物中心的今天。"

黄:"太棒了!你还买了什么?"

朱:"首先,我买了黄色的皮带和一个新的衣服,我一直在寻找自去年夏天。 然后我买的裤子,一个白色的衣服,一件外衣,为我的母亲和一对恤我的父亲。

我离开的时候,我看到一双靴子的裙子储存,并决定买给你。"

黄:"非常感谢,我很感激。"

"今天风很大。"Alessia小姐离开商场时说道。

"这是夏天即将结束的信号。"洛朗先生说。

"我希望我有一件夹克和一双袜子。"

"我想我的包里有一些袜子。"洛朗先生说。

"别担心,我可以在其他服装店买一个,我可以在窗户上看到一些好的眼镜!"

第6章

质询

关键词：What, where, who, why, how many.

问题	Question.
谁？	Who?
为什么呢？	Why?
在哪里？	Where?
多少钱？	How much does this cost?
有多少女孩吃？	How many girls eat?
你吃多少面包？	How much bread do you eat?
多少肉	How much meat?
有多少男孩吃鱼？	How many boys eat fish?
哪只狗？	Which dog?
怎么样？	How?
你怎么写信？	How do you write?
谁读？	Who reads?
它是什么？	What is it?
这是什么？	What's this?
哪一个？	Which one?
蛇在哪里？	Where's the snake?
厨师在哪里？	Where's the cook?
动物园在哪里？	Where is the zoo?
哪个苹果？	Which apple?
这个男孩是谁？	Who is this boy?
汉人是谁？	Who is Han?
你是谁？	Who are you?
你读什么？	What are you reading?
谁喝牛奶？	Who's drinking milk?

训练时间

什么？	Excuse me?
你的企鹅是哪一个？	Which one is your penguin?
哪些男人读报纸？	Which men read the newspaper?
哪个男孩？	Which boy?
我是什么？	What am I?
你的书是哪一本？	Which one is your book?
他为什么迟到？	Why is he late?
哪些龟？	Which turtles?
你有什么问题？	What's your problem?
他读了这个问题	He read the question.
我们有多少本书？	How many books do we have?
问题在哪里？	What's the problem?
你的问题没有答案	Your question has no answer.
你在哪？	Where are you?
你什么时候吃？	When do you eat?
我的回答是否定的	My answer is no.
答案是肯定的	The answer is yes.
从何时起？	Since when?
你和谁一起？	Who are you with?
他多大了？	How old is he?
有多少女孩吃？	How many girls eat?
我有个问题	I have a question.

训练时间

故事模式

ENGLISH

"Hey, Miss Solange! This is Liu Cheng, an advisor on food research. Today, I would like to ask you a few questions if you don't mind."

"Yes, continue."

"Thank you."

"First question, do you eat at least three times a day?"

"Yes."

"When you feel hungry the most?"

"In the morning, this is why I never missed breakfast."

"Where do you eat breakfast?"

"At work."

"What do you like, eggs and meat or vegetarian sandwiches?"

"Eggs and ham, I'm not a vegetarian."

"How do you like eggs? Cooked or fried?"

"I like to boil. Other times, I want to fry."

"What brand of eggs do you buy?"

"SW eggs."

"How many boxes do you buy for a month?"

"Seven."

"How much is a box?"

"Ten dollars."

"Do you see any egg cooking show?"

"Yes. I like the easy way to cook eggs."

"Thank you for your time."

CHINESE

"嘿，小姐Solange! 这是刘成一个顾问在食品研究。 今天，我想问你几个问题如果你不介意的话。"

"肯定的是，继续进行。"

"谢谢你。"

"第一个问题，你至少吃三次一天？"

"是的。"

"当你觉得最饿吗？"

"早上，这就是为什么我从来没有错过早餐。"

"你在哪里吃早餐？"

"在工作方式。"

"你喜欢什么、鸡蛋和肉或素食三明治吗？"

"鸡蛋和火腿，我不是个素食主义者。"

"你怎么喜欢鸡蛋吗？ 煮熟或炸吗？"

"我喜欢煮沸。 其他时候，我要炒。"

"什么牌子的鸡蛋做的，你买什么？"

"SW鸡蛋。"

"多少盒做的你买一个月吗？"

"七。"

"多少是一个盒子？"

"十美元。"

"你看任何蛋烹饪节目?"

"是的。我喜欢简单的方法来煮鸡蛋。"

"谢谢您的时间。"

第7章

动词

关键词： I can, walk, door, do, like, stay, I understand.

我喝	I drink
你好吗？	How are you?
我想要一个番茄汤	I want a tomato soup
不，你不能	No, you can not
谁来到餐厅？	Who came to the restaurant?
你做一个三明治	You make a sandwich
我们有一个厨房	We have a kitchen
他们有书	They have books
我有一把刀	I have a knife
他们是男子汉	They are men
我是一个女孩	I am a girl
你们中有多少人？	How many of you are there?
我们是男孩	We are boys
男人走了	The man is gone
我不知道	I do not know
女人给男孩饼干	The woman gives the boy biscuits
我找不到那个女孩	I can't find the girl
马看到了猫	The horse saw the cat
我认识这些女人	I know these women
男孩打招呼	The boy greets
她拿走我的糖	She took my sugar
咖啡到了	The coffee is coming
她讲	She speaks
他说	He said
我要求一份牛排	I ask for a steak

训练时间

她穿着我的鞋子	She is wearing my shoes
我不把糖放在茶里	I don't put sugar in tea
他们不认为	They do not think
男人们想	The men think
面包何时到达?	When does the bread arrive?
我不懂为什么	I don't understand why
动物仍然留在动物园里	The animals remain in the zoo
我们听到了这只鸟	We heard this bird
她留下了糖果	She left candy
咖啡变甜了	The coffee is sweetened
你在哪里吃面包？	Where do you eat bread?
我们相信	We believe
她离开了那个男孩	She left the boy
我用勺子	I use a spoon
我记得菜单	I remember the menu
他们如何生活?	How do they live?
你吃	You eat
你工作	You work
你等待	You wait
你喝	You drink
你输入?	Did you enter?
你打开书	You open the book
他完成晚餐	He finished his dinner
你如何完成蛋糕？	How do you finish the cake?
我们完成蛋糕	We finish the cake

训练时间

女人吃鱼	The woman eats fish
狮子喜欢肉	The lion likes the meat
我吃一个苹果	I eat an apple
我们喝	We drink
你跟菲利波说话	You talk to Filippo
你需要什么？	You need what?
我们等待饮料	We wait for the beverage
我需要你	I need you
我需要一匹马	I need a horse
我说	I speak
她离开了大衣	She leaves the coat
女人经过那个男人	The woman passes the man
他们需要衣服	They need clothes
她需要一件外套	She needs a coat
我喜欢糖	I like sugar
女孩在等待午餐	The girl waits for lunch
你跟Sara说话	You talk to Sara
我们需要你	We need you
我们不说话	We do not speak
她看起来和读	She looks and reads
她没有找到她的钥匙	She does not find her keys
他带着蛇来到	He arrives with the snake
我们喜欢菠萝	We like pineapples
他带来土豆	He brings potatoes
他带来面包	He brings bread

训练时间

我们跟着你	We follow you
她走	She walks
我原谅你	I forgive you
他们喜欢咖啡	They like coffee
这女孩穿上衣服	The girl is dressed
该男子底下他	The man is under him
他喜欢动物	He likes animals
她停止	She stopped
他试图	He tried
我的回报是附近	My return is nearby
狮子感觉饥饿	The lion feels hungry
他们找到勺子	They found the spoon
我们到达	We arrive
马停下	Stop the horse
我们看看菜单	We look at the menu
他们打开的书	They opened the book
他们喜欢的苹果	They like apples
我可以打开	I can open
我移动	I move
他付	He paid
男孩忘了带来的变化	The boy forgot to bring change
他离开	He is gone
她买鞋子	She buys shoes
他给他的卡	He gave him the card
他睡觉，我做饭	He sleeps and I cook

训练时间

有	Have
写	Write
我跑	I run
你跑	You run
我睡觉	I sleep
他们付钱	They pay
我们睡觉	We sleep
我和建林一起玩	I play with Jianlin
我不买沙拉	I do not buy salad
他们玩	They play
我们和马匹一起玩	We play with horses
她读一本书	She is reading a book
人赢得一个皮带	The man wins a belt
女孩问	The girl asks
我一直幻想	I always fantasize
男人喜欢米胡椒	Men like peppered rice
我展示我的服装	I show my costume
他不会改变	He will not change
他养了农场	He raised the farm
她介绍了秘书	She introduced the secretary
他介绍了这位女士	He introduced this lady
他不存在	He does not exist
他们在晚上出现	They appear at night
女孩尝试汤	The girl tries soup
你把咖啡给主任	You give coffee to the director

训练时间

我梦想着书	I dream of a book
他生产洋葱	He produces onions
他们品尝米饭	They taste rice
学生展示他们的工作	Students show their work
他们生产面包	They produce bread
这是很熟悉	This is very familiar
她依靠她的家人	She relies on her family
她寻找她的母亲	She searches for her mother
午餐开始在一分钟	Lunch starts in one minute
他不算数	He does not count
我尊重司机	I respect the driver
鞋子不适合	The shoes are not suitable
截止日期在周五结束	Deadline ends on Friday
我们依靠你	We rely on you
我今天开始	I started today
他们似乎很自然	They seem natural
我们尊重你的一代	We respect your generation
她的签名	Her signature
你为什么不进来?	Why don't you come in?
他供应米饭	He serves rice
门不关闭	The door does not close
派对依赖于建筑师	The party depends on the architect
我们偷走了婴儿床	We stole the crib

你来的时候无所谓	It doesn't matter when you come
他们签署了这本书	They signed the book

训练时间

男孩关上窗户	The boy closes the window
他们导入你的结构	They import your structure
我在哪里签字?	Where do I sign?
他供应咖啡	He serves coffee
门不关	The door is not closed
你选择尺寸	You choose the size
如果他听到你的话	If he hears you
房子里有一只狗	There is a dog in the house
他提交了一个答案	He submitted an answer
你坐在地板上吗?	Are you sitting on the floor?
我的孩子学得很快	My child is learning quickly
我们转向老师	We turn to the teacher
我听你说话	I listen to you
他们不听吗?	Do they not listen?
我的妹妹学习颜色	My sister learns colors
一个女孩回答	One girl answered
你撒谎	You are lying
他解释了这个行业	He explained this industry
你喜欢苹果还是香蕉?	Do you like apples or bananas?
我不撒谎	I don't lie

我给他提供果汁	I give him juice
动物不撒谎	Animals do not lie
我移动冰箱	I move the refrigerator
男孩成长	The boys grow
婴儿的哭声	The baby cries

训练时间

我同意	I agree
我们同意	We agree
我唱歌	I sing
我飞	I fly
我学习	I learn
他笑了	He laughed
明天我解释为什么	Tomorrow, I explain why
我们建立一个家庭	We build a family
我们感谢法官	We thank the judge
他们在下午学习	They study in the afternoon
她住在一所大房子里	She lives in a big house
我们击中了一个男人	We hit a man
秘书提供咖啡	The secretary provides coffee
刀子撞到墙上	The knife hit the wall
他们住在一个大房子里	They live in a big house
我提供她的意大利面	I offer her spaghetti
刀命一个人	The knife killed a man
我们烧饼	We bake
女孩们一起学习	The girls learn together
我想是这样	I think so

邮递员是在旅途中与他的女儿	The postman is on a journey with his daughter
母亲教她的孩子	The mother teaches her child
我送食物	I send food
女人醒了	The woman woke up
他看着鸟儿	He looks at the birds

训练时间

他们设置了桌子	They set the table
鞋子伤害了女孩	The shoes hurt the girl
我今天训练	I train today
她设置了桌子	She set the table
他提供食物	He provides food
我照顾我的祖父	I take care of my grandfather
他训练这个男孩	He trains this boy
鸟在卧室里飞行	Birds fly in the bedroom
我们像婴儿一样哭泣	We cry like babies
他把钥匙放在口袋里	He put the key in his pocket
他日夜学习	He studied day and night
你喜欢米饭还是面包？	Do you like rice or bread?
母亲把婴儿裹在毯子里	The mother wraps the baby in a blanket
家人邀请作家去吃晚饭	The family invited the writer to dinner
你看到了什么？	What do you see?
我们烧饭	We cook
我们不睡觉	We do not sleep

你吼他们	You see them
他们推迟午餐	They postponed lunch
不，你不走	No, you don't go
他们烧汤	They cook soup
我不支付	I do not pay
他们失败了	They failed
我们失败了很多次	We failed many times
我没有失败	I did not fail

训练时间

他们在哪里保持盐？	Where do they keep the salt?
灯泡烫了毛巾	The lamp burns the towel
他认为我们是人类	He thinks we are human
姐妹们移动镜子	The sisters move the mirror
建筑师移动灯	The architect moves the lamp
我用油填满瓶子	I filled the bottle with oil
法官判断主教	The judge judges the bishop
她住在我家	She lives in my house
她改进了菜单	She improved the menu
她带着梯子	She is carrying a ladder
他们煮鸡蛋	They cook eggs
他吃午饭	He had lunch
我听不到	I can not hear
他们带着书	They carry books
鸟不会游泳	Birds can't swim

她不骑马	She does not ride horses
他照顾动物	He takes care of animals
他们有书	They have books
你提供食物	You provide food
我们不跑	We don't run
我们想要苹果	We want apples
是的，我去	Yes, I go
我吃面包	I eat bread
男孩们喝水	The boys drink water
我问一个问题	I ask a question

训练时间

我们去	Let's go
我们可以吗?	Can we?
我可以	I can
您可以	You can
你不做饭鸭?	Don't you cook duck?
我爸爸会游泳，你妈妈会走路	My dad can swim and your mother can walk
孩子们看到了熊。	The children saw the bear
丈夫吻了妻子	The husband kissed his wife
我用水填满瓶子	I filled the bottle with water
我有一只动物，它是一只老鼠	I have an animal, it is a mouse
你想要哪件连衣裙?	Which dress do you want?
韩想要一只粉红色的蜘蛛	Han wants a pink spider

你为午餐付钱	You pay for lunch
不，你不去	No, you don't go
汉睡觉，黄运行	Han sleeps, Huang runs
我们推出一份新报纸	We launch a new newspaper
狗玩耍	The dog plays
孩子们不支付	Children do not pay
男孩不走	The boy does not walk
她走了，我走了	She is gone, I am gone
男孩们听着	The boys are listening
我们不支付	We do not pay
那人指着那匹马	The man pointed at the horse
我们做酱	We make sauce
我找到了狗	I found the dog

训练时间

知道	Know
找	Find
游戏	Game
样品	Sample
下雨了	It's raining
我知道	I know
鸟不说话	The bird does not speak
你不要碰洋葱	Don't touch the onions
他们尖叫着你的名字	They scream your name
我们不碰这只鸡	We do not touch the chicken
大象想要水	The elephant wants water
猫没有听到	The cat did not hear
她说话，他们说话	She speaks, they speak

他们研究这些书	They study these books
我们找到食物	We find food
孩子玩耍	The children play
我不知道	I do not know
没有盐了	No salt
他们跟随他们的父亲	They follow their father
女人尝尝面包	The woman tastes bread
你展示你的腰带	You show your belt
我梦见我的女朋友	I dreamt of my girlfriend
他们在晚上出现	They appear at night
我寻找我的狗	I am looking for my dog
他们展示他们的家庭	They show their family

训练时间

我们帮助	We help
回去！	Go back!
我的阿姨是孤独的	My aunt is lonely
黄关闭了窗户	Huang closed the window
我在你和他之间	I am between you and him
他们很安全	They are safe
我们正在吃晚饭	We are eating dinner
我们记得我们的祖母	We remember our grandmother
她寻找她的猫	She is looking for her cat
她关上了门	She closed the door
哪个梦想？	Which dream?
我想到你	I think of you

他们不给食物	They don't give food
狗帮助那个人	The dog helps that person
厨师称肉	The chef weighs meat
她看着窗户	She looks at the window
他和女孩在一起	He is with the girl
他们尝试大米	They try rice
我weigh我的儿子	I weigh my son
他显示了这些信件	He showed these letters
我们看看菜单	We look at the menu
我接受沙发	I accept the sofa
我尊重女性	I respect women
他不接受	He does not accept
她拿走我的糖	She took my sugar

训练时间

她访问她的家人	She visits her family
他们喝酒	They drink
我们认为不是	We think not
她给水	She gives water
我带着我的狗回来	I came back with my dog
他尊重他的妻子	He respects his wife
他访问了医生	He visited a doctor
她拿着帽子	She is holding a hat
熊不适合通过门	The bear does not fit through the door
是的，它似乎很熟悉	Yes, it seems familiar
她明天开始	She will start tomorrow
他为大米服务	He serves rice

你去过北京？	Have you been to Beijing?
你不算数	You don't count
这个月在星期一结束	This month ends on Monday
你认识我的女儿	You know my daughter
鞋子不适合	The shoes do not fit
我明天开始	I will start tomorrow
他们似乎很自然	They seem natural
他计数三明治	He counts sandwiches
我们为晚餐服务	We serve dinner
他在书上签名	He signed the book
九月结束	The end of September
母亲责怪孩子	The mother blames the child
她递交了这封信	She submitted this letter

训练时间

他对她有什么感觉?	How does he feel about her?
他们进口他的婴儿床	They imported his crib
他包括他的母亲	He includes his mother
他进入厨房	He enters the kitchen
他们在书上签名	They signed the book
我送食物	I send food
不，颜色并不重要	No, color is not important
他们包括一件不同的衣服	They include a different dress
我进口奶酪	I import cheese
我们签了他的衬衫	We signed his shirt
妈妈，请进来	Mom, please come in

取决于	It depends
他说	He said
明天可以开始	Tomorrow can begin
我们打开这本书	We open this book
我丈夫迟到了	My husband is late
它需要工作	It needs work
我说是	I say yes
你打开门	You open the door
我们明天到达	We will arrive tomorrow
农民们说这本书很好	Farmers say this book is very good
他们什么时候到达?	When will they arrive?
他需要更多的食物	He needs more food
你什么时候回来?	When will you come back?
我不买它	I don't buy it

训练时间

我打开果汁	I open the juice
画家依赖于他	The painter relies on him
你喜欢夏天吗?	Do you like summer?
他不怀疑它	He does not doubt it
我们很晚才回来	We came back late
她要求一个苹果	She asks for an apple
我救了我的邻居	I saved my neighbor
我不喜欢那些电话	I don't like those phones
这个男孩买了一只狗	The boy bought a dog
她装满了瓶子	She is filled with bottles
我怀疑,他怀疑	I doubt that he doubts

我们拯救动物	We save animals
这班车停在天津吗？	Is this bus parked in Tianjin?
他继续他的文件	He continues his document
他赢了二十美元	He won twenty dollars
我问他	I asked him
他混合洋葱	He mixes onions
她拥有一辆红色的汽车	She owns a red car
他不问	He doesn't ask
我站在街上	I stand on the street
他们混合果汁和牛奶	They mix juice and milk
我住在一个城市	I live in a city
他们继续	They continue
你赚了很多钱	You make a lot of money
你问同样的事情	You ask the same thing

训练时间

你允许狗吗？	Do you allow dogs?
谁收到兔子？	Who received the rabbit?
他认为我是朋友	He thinks that I am a friend
他们用糖	They use sugar
他加了盐的到汤。	He added salt to the soup.
这辆车很值钱	This car is very valuable
你住在哪里？	Where do you live?
我的搭档允许	My partner allows it
你使用电脑	You use a computer

他们认为我是朋友	They think I'm a friend
他住在德国	He lives in Germany
我们住在这里	We live here
他认识她	He knows her
我花钱	I spend money
他不了解我	He doesn't understand me
她没有回答我	She did not answer me
三明治包含奶酪	The sandwich contains cheese
他击败了他的朋友	He defeated his friend
这让很多人感兴趣	This makes many people interested
我不明白	I do not understand
他们击败了他们的敌人	They defeated their enemies
我花了太多	I spent too much
你不明白我的意思	You don't understand what I mean
我砍苹果	I cut the apple
你预定一张桌子	You book a table

训练时间

我休息	I rest
我唱歌	I sing
我跳	I jump
我飞	I fly
我开车	I will drive
我开着车	I drive a car
我拒绝他	I refuse him
他处理孩子	He handles children
她改进了菜单	She improved the menu
我观察他	I observe him

他伸手去拿帽子	He reached for his hat
他影响我	He influences me
你身上发生了什么?	What happened to you?
我咨询了我的老板	I consulted my boss
我想要一个儿子	I want a son
他保留了桌子	He kept the table
我们一起度过这一天	We spend this day together
她失去了她的钥匙	She lost her key
我不这么认为	I do not think so
孩子们经过这里	Children go through here
我把酒传给我母亲	I passed the wine to my mother
你认出他的衬衫	You recognize his shirt
该玻璃含有水	The glass contains water
我的女儿希望有一匹马	My daughter wants a horse
他观察他的女儿	He observed his daughter

训练时间

现在，他会尝试这个	Now he will try this
多少钱?	How much is it?
啤酒多少钱?	How much is beer?
他咨询安德烈	He consults Andrea
他把食物留在我家里	He left food in my home
他表现得很好	He performed well
他们设置了桌子	They set the table
她创建一个菜单	She creates a menu
那只鸟不飞	The bird does not fly

鸟儿飞	Birds fly
我可以在这里	I can be here
你永远不会输	You will never lose
他是不是好风	He is not good for Feng
我使用伦敦地铁	I use London Underground
我叫王	My name is king
这个月明天结束	This month ends tomorrow
她认为已经晚了	She thinks it's too late
他和我的妹妹走在一起	He walked with my sister
他在这里	He's here
你不属于这里	You don't belong here
你不相信我	You do not believe me
我干这件衬衫	I do this shirt
她和我的朋友一起走	She walks with my friends
他跌倒了	He fell
提起盘子	Lift the tray

训练时间

感觉	Feel
转到这里	Go here
射击场	Shooting range
我们决定	We decide
我的儿子不恨你	My son does not hate you
他干了他的鞋子	He dried his shoes
医生治好了我	The doctor cured me
我不需要我的信件	I don't need my letter
他们提供更多的钱	They provide more money

他们每天都出去	They go out every day
我不需要更多的肉	I don't need more meat
我的母亲使用烤箱	My mother uses the oven
我讨厌星期一	I hate Monday
她七点起床	She gets up at seven
我干我的衬衫	I dry my shirt
火车九点离开	The train leaves at nine
她需要它	She needs it
我明天离开	I am leaving tomorrow
她给我开了她的车	She opened her car for me
他等了五年	He waited five years
我丢弃了食物	I discarded the food
我们需要一张桌子	We need a table
你等待午餐	You are waiting for lunch
我们不认识那个女孩	We don't know the girl
猫喜欢牛奶	The cat likes milk

训练时间

故事模式

ENGLISH

Today is the first day of spring. The boys, Han and Bo, decided to meet friends at the lakeside bar to celebrate the new season. Zhao wanted to go with them, but they did not agree because he was too young to drink. On their way, the boys saw a bear walking towards them. If Zhao was here, he may have fainted, but the boys wait for the bear to leave quietly. Shortly after, the boys entered the bar and watched the argument in front of them.

"The man pays, I dance, I don't pay," Adriana shouted.

"It is impossible to have two, Adriana. We cannot pay salaries and still give drinks and food free." said the person in charge of the bar.

"No problem, we will pay all the fees." Han said.

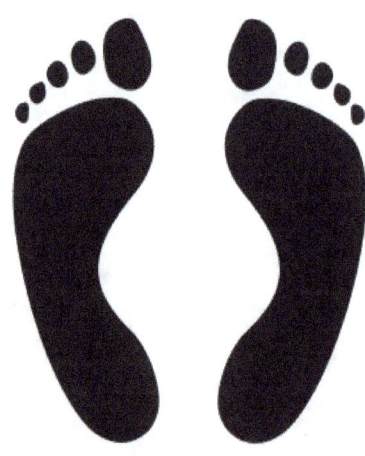

CHINESE

今天是春天的第一天．孩子们，汉和博，决定满足的朋友在湖边的酒吧为了庆祝新一季的。赵想和他们一起去，但他们并没有同意，因为他太年轻饮酒。上他们的方式，孩子们看到了一个熊走向他们。如果赵在这里，他可能会晕倒，但这些男孩静静地等着熊离开．此后不久，男孩进入酒吧，在他们面前观看了争论。

"男人支付的，我跳舞，我不付出，"阿德里安娜喊道。

这是不可能有两个，阿德里安娜．我们不能支付薪金和还是给饮料和食品免费。"酒吧的负责人说。

"没问题，我们将付出的一切."说汉。

第8章

介词

关键词：From, in, to, on, with.

他们写信给女性	They write to women
男孩们读给男人听	The boys read to the men
我们把面包给鸭子	We give bread to the duck
这个女孩不喜欢果汁	This girl does not like juice
谁来动物园	Who comes to the zoo?
他们在吃午饭	They are having lunch
我们正在吃晚饭	We are eating dinner
我想起了丽莎	I think of Lisa
我在动物园	I am at the zoo
他住在墨西哥	He lives in Mexico
谁相信孩子？	Who believes in children?
他们写了关于她	They wrote about her
油在瓶子里	The oil is in the bottle
我喝橙汁	I drink orange juice
我在报纸上	I am in the newspaper
他在厨房里做饭	He cooks in the kitchen
我想要一盘米饭	I want a plate of rice
我们从眼镜喝	We drink from glasses
我来自动物园	I come from the zoo
肉来自动物	Meat comes from animals
食物在盘子里	Food in the plate
我写的食谱	The recipe I wrote

牛奶来自牛	Milk comes from cows
我走向马	I went to the horse
这是给她的	This is for her

训练时间

到什么时候？	When?
叉子在盘子上	Fork on a plate
蚂蚁在糖上	Ants on sugar
柠檬水在瓶子里	Lemonade in a bottle
我们相信男人	We believe in men
据男孩说，她不吃鸡肉	According to the boy, she does not eat chicken
她来自餐厅	She comes from the restaurant
我们把糖放在蛋糕上	We put sugar on the cake
我们从男孩那里买水果	We buy fruit from the boy
鱼生活在水中	Fish live in water
他们在我们之间	They are between us
我用盐煮鱼。	I use salt to cook fish.
他看着你	He looks at you
鸡蛋不在盘子上	Eggs are not on the plate
我向他走去	I walked to him
据她介绍，这不是一条鱼	According to her, this is not a fish
肉来自鸭子	Meat comes from ducks
除了酒	In addition to wine
除了啤酒	In addition to beer
我有男人的盘子	I have a man's plate

她吃没有油的沙拉	She eats salad without oil
他有马	He has horses
我们谈论书籍	We talk about books
我问他	I asked him
你想要一些糖吗?	Do you want some sugar?

训练时间

我们住在水边	We live by the water
蜘蛛是墙上的	The spider is on the wall
这些书来自女性	These books are from women
我们在晚餐时喝葡萄酒	We drank wine at dinner
尽管颜色不同，我们仍然购买鞋子	Despite the different colors, we still buy shoes
我们用鸡肉吃米饭	We eat rice with chicken
我吃水果，除了苹果	I eat fruit, except apples
你不带糖加咖啡吗?	Don't you have sugar and coffee?
靴子的颜色是什么?	What is the color of the boots?
女孩的猫是白色的	The girl's cat is white
蚂蚁在橙色	Ants in orange
女孩的鞋子是黑色的	The girl's shoes are black
这不是男人的叉路口	This is not a man's fork

训练时间

第9章

日期和时间

关键词：Week, month, second, year, date, time.

晚	Night
天	Day
日期	Date
日历	Calendar
从七月到九月	From July to September
四月份结束今天	April ends today
三月在二月到四月之间	March is between February and April
明天见！	See you tomorrow!
我们在一月份	We are in January
这是昨天的面包	This is yesterday's bread
我在一月份和他一起吃晚饭	I had dinner with him in January
昨天是男人，今天是女人	Yesterday it was a man and today it is a woman
他们在二月吃什么？	What do they eat in February?
三月今天结束	March ends today
现在是八月	It is August
现在是十一月	It is now November
可能今天不会结束	May does not end today
明天是星期四	Tomorrow is Thursday
我们在十月给他们写信	We wrote to them in October
这是一个星期一	This is a Monday
你星期六工作吗？	Do you work on Saturday?

周二我吃奶酪	I eat cheese on Tuesday
今天是星期一	Today is Monday
今天是周六	Today is Saturday
他在十二月去世	He died in December

训练时间

春天	Spring
冬天	Winter
我星期五吃牛排	I eat steak on Friday
周三我们吃奶酪	We eat cheese on Wednesday
今天是星期五	Today is Friday
餐厅于六月开业	The restaurant opened in June
我和他一起度过了这个夏天	I spent this summer with him
我早上喝咖啡	I drink coffee in the morning
今天是星期日	Today is Sunday
我在中午吃饭	I eat at noon
狗喜欢秋天	Dogs like autumn
这个蛋糕是为了星期天	This cake is for Sunday
在伦敦是春天	In London it is spring
我在下午吃巧克力	I eat chocolate in the afternoon
我在晚上工作	I work at night
他工作到午夜	He works until midnight
周五和周六晚上	Friday and Saturday nights
现在是蛋糕的时候了	It's time for cake
我们今晚去哪里?	Where are we going tonight?
稍等一会儿!	Wait a moment!
我今晚工作	I work tonight
我在晚上工作	I work at night

分钟和小时过去了	Minutes and hours have passed
本月的几周	Week of the month
星期二是一周中的一天	Tuesday is a day of the week

训练时间

秒通过	The seconds pass
这是晚餐时间	It is dinner time
能打扰你几分钟吗？	Can i bother you for a few minutes?
我等不及了	I can not wait anymore
我们每小时喝一瓶	We drink a bottle every hour
一个世纪不是一年	A century is not a year
在一个月	In a month
分钟和小时过去了	Minutes and hours have passed
十年今天结束	The decade ends today
晚会是明天	The party is tomorrow
明天是我的生日	Tomorrow is my birthday
该时期在四月结束	The period ended in April
几年或几个月？	Years or months?
几个世纪过去了	The centuries pass
他们工作了几十年	They worked for decades
今天几号？	What is today's date?
你今天早上迟到了	You arrived late this morning
天色已晚	It's late
再见！	Goodbye!
我没时间	I do not have time
一个月前	One month ago

他每周与我们一起吃饭	He eats with us every week
你今天早上喝什么？	What did you drink this morning?
这个女人有一个日历	The woman has a calendar
春天是一个季节	Spring is a season

训练时间

分钟和秒	Minutes and seconds
一天中的几小时	Hours of the day
几个星期和几个月	Weeks and months
破晓	Breaking dawn
本赛季	This season
在夜晚	At night
多少分钟?	How many minutes?
他星期四到达	He arrived on Thursday
起点在哪里？	Where is the starting point?
八月和九月是一年中的几个月	August and September are months of the year
我在那个时期工作	I worked in that period
我早上走路	I walk in the morning
今天几号？	What's the date today?
他们去参加节日	They go to the festival
我星期一不工作	I do not work on Monday
我不会在十月份跑	I will not run in October
一分钟是一瞬间	One minute is a moment
夏天是为了青春	Summer is for youth
她的周年是七月	Her anniversary is July.
世纪的诞生	The birth of the century

周期有多长？	How long is the cycle?
这些字母没有日期	There are no dates for these letters
一天中的秒数	The number of seconds in a day
冬天很长	Winter is long
星期一，星期二和星期三	Monday, Tuesday and Wednesday

训练时间

我的儿子赵是一岁。	My son Zhao is one year old.
我需要一秒钟	I need a second
上星期六，我们吃肉	Last Saturday, we ate meat
有时是的，有时没有	Sometimes yes, sometimes no
阿尔贝托星期一，星期二和星期三喝啤酒	Alberto drinks beer on Monday and Wednesday
我们没有日期	We have no date
我的阿姨丽迪雅昨天来了	My aunt Lydia came yesterday
十月和十二月是一年中的几个月	October and December are months of the year
三月，四月，五月和六月	March, April, May and June
我的祖母在二月份不跑	My grandmother does not run in February
五月的一个星期五	One Friday in May
截至今日	As of today
他在十一月写道	He wrote in November
八月份我不吃鱼	I don't eat fish in August
从九月到十二月	From September to December

冬天是一个季节	Winter is a season
我们吃了一会儿	We ate for a while
各方不是明天	All parties are not tomorrow
我早上走路	I walk in the morning
假期在八月	Holidays in August
我在中午吃饭	I eat at noon
我今天和她约会	I dated her today

训练时间

故事模式

ENGLISH

"January, February and March are the best months of my work."

"Why do you say that?"

"Because the rainy season is over in January. It is easier to clean up the ground and the grass is dry. Weeds cannot grow quickly.

Iron and cement prices will fall in February, and I can buy more at lower prices. In March, I earn a little more, which helps speed up the work."

"I see, what about the other months?"

"In April, the price of stone was cheaper. Work begins in mid-June, and the rainy season begins from July to August. The rain is most intense in September and October, and in December, we take a break."

CHINESE

"一月，二月和三月是我工作中最好的几个月。"

"你为什么这么说？"

"因为雨季结束在一月份.而且清理地面更容易施工，草地干燥，杂草不能迅速生长。

铁和水泥价格将下降在二月，和我可以买到更多的价格较低的。在三月，我赚得多一点，这有助于加快工作"

"我明白了，什么有关的其他个月？"

"月份的石头价格更便宜，工作开始于六月中，和雨季开始从七月至八月

在九月和十月的,雨是最激烈，和在十二月，我们休息一下。"

11/18/2018

第10章

家庭

关键词：Father, mother, children, uncle, cousin, sisters.

家庭	Family
父亲	Father
母亲	Mother
儿子	Son
女儿	Daughter
孩子	Child
那个兄弟	The brother
姐妹	Sisters
爷爷	Grandfather
祖母	Grandmother
丈夫	Husband
宝宝	Baby
他和我的母亲是哥哥和妹妹。	He and my mother are brother and sister.
我想要个儿子和一个女儿。	I want a son and a daughter.
我们是兄弟姐妹	We are brothers and sisters
我的父亲有一家餐馆	My father has a restaurant
我的父母吃米饭	My parents eat rice
我的女儿想要一只手表	My daughter wants a watch
我母亲的姐妹们不吃鸡肉	My mother's sisters do not eat chicken
他们是我的兄弟	They are my brothers
我有一个妹妹	I have a younger sister
他们的孩子喝牛奶	Their children drink milk

我们是夫妻	We are husband and wife
我们是表兄弟	We are cousins
他不是我的表弟	He is not my cousin

训练时间

祖父你好！	Hello grandfather!
我叔叔的妻子是我的阿姨	My uncle's wife is my aunt
他们是妻子	They are the wives
我们去奶奶的	We go to grandma's
我和我的阿姨一起吃饭	I eat with my aunt
果汁是给我奶奶的	The juice is for my grandma
妈妈，爸爸在哪里？	Where is Mommy and Daddy?
我们有名字和姓氏	We have a first name and a last name
我们怎么写她的姓？	How do we write her last name?
你就像你的妈妈	You are like your mother
感谢爸爸！	Thanks dad!
她就像她的妈妈	She is like her mother
你姓什么？	What is your last name?
我的侄女有一只狗	My niece has a dog
那个男孩的狗	The boy's dog
我们有一个儿子和一只猫	We have a son and a cat
我们是他的孩子	We are his children
你的父母是谁？	Who are your parents?
赵不是你的父亲	Zhao is not your father
我的孩子来自意大利	My child is from Italy
韩和宝是我的儿子	Han Hebao is my son

黄不是我的母亲	Huang is not my mother
安德烈不是我的父亲	Andre is not my father
是的，阿尔贝托是我的丈夫	Yes, Alberto is my husband.
达芬奇是我的兄弟	Leonardo da Vinci is my brother

训练时间

我是他的妻子	I am his wife
他们是我的叔叔	They are my uncles
她是我姑妈	She is my aunt
她和我的母亲是姐妹	She and my mother are sisters.
你是我们的妻子	You are our wife
不，你没有婴儿	No, you do not have babies
我的母亲是一位祖母	My mother is a grandmother
奇科是我的祖父	Chico is my grandfather
我的祖母是罗莎	My grandmother is Rosa.
我的家人来自德国	My family is from Germany
谢谢奶奶	Thank you Grandma
蓝帽子是给我的祖母	The blue hat is for my grandmother
他不是我的表弟	He is not my cousin
韩和宝是我的表兄弟	Han Hebao is my cousin
赵是我的表弟	Zhao is my cousin
这顶白帽子不适合我的祖母	This white hat is not suitable for my grandmother
我们是表兄弟	We are cousins

阿尔贝托和索尼娅生了一个孩子	Alberto and Sonia had a child
我的妻子是我儿子的母亲	My wife is the mother of my son
说完之后，他和他的妻子离开了	After speaking, he and his wife left
汤是给莱昂纳多的	The soup is for Leonardo

训练时间

故事模式

ENGLISH

Zhu: "Your sister Yifeng just sent a photo to Instagram. There are many people inside and it looks like a great family portrait."

Huang: "Yes, a photographer came to our house today. We took pictures to celebrate my grandfather's birthday."

"On the left are my brother and his wife, they are married and have just returned from their honeymoon, and on the right of them is my father, whom you have met countless times."

"This is the youngest member of the family, my niece Stella. She's just a girl, but she's very pretty."

"Sitting next to my grandfather was my grandmother, my mother, my uncle and my lawyer. And on the floor, we have my cousin and my nephew."

Zhu: "This is a great family photo."

Huang: "I know, I like it."

CHINESE

朱："你姐姐Yifeng刚刚给Instagram发了一张照片。 里面有很多人，看起来像一幅伟大的全家福。"

黄： "是的，一位摄影师今天来到我们家，我们拍了照片来庆祝我的祖父的生日。"

"左边是我的兄弟和他的妻子，他们刚结婚和他们刚回来从蜜月，我父亲在右边，你有见过他许多次。"

"这是这个家庭中最小的成员，我的侄女斯特拉，她只是一个女孩，但她非常漂亮。"

"坐在旁边我的祖父是我的祖母，我的母亲，我的叔叔和我的律师。

"和在地板上，我们有我的表弟和我的侄子。"

朱："这是一张很棒的家庭照片。"

黄："我知道，我喜欢它。"

第Ⅱ章

颜色

关键词： Colored, black, white, red, yellow, blue.

颜色是绿色的	The color is green
这件毛衣是蓝色的	This sweater is blue
一件彩色的衬衫	A colored shirt
我们买黑裤子	We buy black pants
这个女人有一条棕色腰带	This woman has a brown belt
她的袜子是灰色的	Her socks are gray
鞋子是蓝色的	Shoes are blue
橙色	Orange
羊毛是紫色的	The wool is purple
鸟是黄色的	The bird is yellow
我的衬衫是白色的	My shirt is white
她有红色的裤子	She has red pants
这只猫不是白色的	This cat is not white

我的白衬衫在哪里？	Where is my white shirt?
她的衣服是黑色的	Her clothes are black
这件外套是粉红色的	The coat is pink
大象是灰色的	The elephant is grey
我不知道你最喜欢的颜色	I don't know your favorite color
她穿着红色的裤子	She is wearing red pants
它是一样的颜色	It is the same color
她的衬衫是绿色的	Her shirt is green
我喜欢黑色的裙子	I like black skirts
罐头是白色的	The cans are white
绳子是棕色的	The rope is brown
紫色手套	Purple gloves

第12章

职业

关键词：Work, clown, conductor, captain, architect, mechanic, director, workers, secretary, researchers, doctor, model, soldier, police.

学生	The student
船长	Captain
守卫	Guard
作者	Author
作家	Writer
艺术家	Artist
该模型	The model
权威	Authority
医生	Doctors
战士	Warrior

国王	King
王子	Prince
农民	Farmers
建筑师	The architect
研究人员	The researchers
画家	Painter
专业人员	The professionals
主教	Bishop
法官	Judge
老师	The teacher
读者	Reader
学生	The student
代表	Representative
企业家	The entrepreneur
警察	Policemen

训练时间

校长	The principal
他是工程师，她是建筑师	He is an engineer and she is an architect
农民与牛和鸡一起工作	The farmers work with cattle and chickens
工程师说什么？	What does the engineer say?
她是一名渔夫	She is a fisherman
他与警卫谈话	He talks with the guard
你是主持人吗？	Are you the host?
你是一个小丑	You are a clown
农民读取该报	The farmers read the newspaper
我们的兄弟是机械师	Our brother is a mechanic
警察有蓝色衬衫	The police have blue shirts

水管工吃什么？	What does a plumber eat?
我们不是邮递员	We are not postmen
你的律师是谁？	Who is your lawyer?
我的妹妹没有工作	My sister did not work
经理在哪里？	Where is the manager?
谁是工人？	Who is the worker?
我去看医生	I went to see a doctor
炸鱼是你的特长	Fish is your specialty
我的丈夫不是秘书	My husband is not a secretary
我的丈夫是研究员	My husband is a researcher
我的叔叔和我的阿姨是医生	My uncle and my aunt are doctors
我认识一位研究员	I know a researcher
作者写道	The author wrote
渔夫喝一杯咖啡。	The fisherman drinks a cup of coffee.

训练时间

船长的回答今天到来	The captain's answer arrived today
你的父亲是农民	Your father is a farmer
你是一名建筑师	You are an architect
我的母亲等待邮递员	My mother waits for the postman
她的职业是什么？	What is her career?
她是我的顾问	She is my advisor
答案是就业	The answer is employment
观众想要柠檬水	The audience wants lemonade
观众星期四抵达	The audience arrived on Thursday

专家与国王说话	The expert speaks with the king
我需要一名律师	I need a lawyer
他是警方的发言人	He is a spokesman for the police
他是本世纪的领袖	He is the leader of this century
我不是记者	I am not a reporter
上校和导演说话	The colonel and director speak
晚安，伯爵夫人	Good night, Countess
我是日内瓦代表	I am a representative of Geneva
老师看到他们的学生	The teacher sees their students
他们是领导者	They are leaders
他们是艺术家	They are artists
她是一名教师	She is a teacher
你是模特儿吗？	Are you a model?
他是一名商人	He is a businessman
你是医生	You are a doctor
学生们吃饭	The students eat

训练时间

面包	Bread
艺术家	The artist
王子	The prince
勺子是为国王	The spoon is for the king
我的母亲和我的阿姨是老师	My mother and my aunt are teachers
学生喝水	The students drink water
他是学生	He is a student

作家喝葡萄酒。	The writer drinks wine.
他与医生交谈	He talks with the doctor
老师早上好	Good morning teacher
萨拉和克里斯蒂娜是女警察	Sarah and Christina are policewomen
老师吃三明治	The teacher eats a sandwich
检察官是谁？	Who is the prosecutor?
他们是模特儿	They are models
他是一名秘书	He is a secretary
我们是老师	We are teachers
我需要一个医生	I need a doctor
学生们吃面包	The students eat bread
你有多少个老板？	How many bosses do you have?
她是我的秘书	She is my secretary
弗雷多是一名警察	Fredo is a policeman
你有一个秘书	You have a secretary
皇后不喝啤酒	The queen does not drink beer
老师吃苹果	The teacher eats apple
她是我的老板	She is my boss

训练时间

画家	The painter
农民	The farmers
厨师	The chef
我是一名记者	I am a reporter
他与警卫谈话	He talks with the guard
诗人写了一封信	The poet wrote a letter
我的叔叔是这本书的作者	My uncle is the author of this book
我是个商人	I am a businessman

教授们阅读	The professors read
我不是教授	I am not a professor
帕特里夏是法官	Patricia is a judge
士兵吃饭	The soldiers eat
你是作者吗?	Are you an author?
我的父亲是一位诗人	My father is a poet
我们是教授	We are professors
我的叔叔是一名雇员	My uncle is an employee
你的律师是谁?	Who is your lawyer?
上校与士兵谈话	The colonel talks with the soldiers
不，佩德罗不是演员，他是一位诗人	No, Pedro is not an actor. He is a poet.
他们是艺术家	They are artists
我有一位律师	I have a lawyer
他的雇员写信	His employees write letters
安杰洛和赵是艺术家	Angelo and Zhao are artists
厨师吃肉	The chef eats meat
我的妹妹是我的律师	My sister is my lawyer

训练时间

我是狗的主人	I am the owner of the dog
谁是代理人?	Who is the agent?
他们是专家	They are experts
指挥官吃橙子	The commander eats oranges
肉是他们的专长	Meat is their specialty

艺术家和画家	Artists and painters
主人有一匹马	The owner has a horse
我的母亲是鸟类专家	My mother is a bird expert
是的，我是一名工程师和一名木匠	Yes, I am an engineer and a carpenter
是的，我的叔叔魏是代理人	Yes, my uncle Wei is an agent
实践很重要	Practice is very important
是的，韩是面包师	Yes, Han is a baker
我是一名教师	I am a teacher
他们是出纳员	They are tellers
她是我的护士吗？	Is she my nurse?
这不是我的专业	This is not my profession
保罗是一位牧师	Paul is a priest
她是面包师	She is a baker
他们是收银员	They are cashiers
他们不是运动员	They are not athletes
一位牧师不喝啤酒	A priest does not drink beer
女祭司有一只黑猫	The priestess has a black cat
我女儿是女服务员	My daughter is a waitress
我的叔叔不是农民，他是面包师	My uncle is not a farmer. He is a baker.

训练时间

工人	Worker
水管工人	Plumber
邮差	Postman
小丑	Clown

祭司们写书	Priests write books
我的女朋友是司机	My girlfriend is a driver
我是一名服务员	I am a waiter
不，我的兄弟大卫不是木匠	No, my brother David is not a carpenter
他的配偶是一名司机	His spouse is a driver
宝不是工程师，他是护士	Bao is not an engineer, he is a nurse
你的叔叔不是护士，他是厨师	Your uncle is not a nurse. He is a chef
不，狮子座和索菲亚不是运动员	No, Leo and Sofia are not athletes
哈里是一位英国工程师	Harry is a British engineer
卡洛斯不是演员，他是学生	Carlos is not an actor, he is a student
他谈到他的原则	He talks about his principles
你有一个很好的记忆	You have a good memory
她向我解释了这些条款	She explained these terms to me
他以邮递员的身份工作	He works as a postman
秘书喝咖啡。	The secretary drinks coffee.
我的女儿是一名女警察	My daughter is a policewoman
这是我们的专长	This is our expertise
我的叔叔是主持人	My uncle is the host
我们不是邮递员	We are not postmen
我是一名警察	I am a police officer

训练时间

故事模式

ENGLISH

Rodrigo: "Where do your parents work?"

Luca: "My father is a lawyer and my mother is also a lawyer."

Rodrigo: "And your siblings?"

Luca: "My older sister works as a secretary, while my brother is a painter."

Rodrigo: "And you?"

Luca: "So far I have published two books, so I can call myself an author."

Rodrigo: "Do you want to be anything else when you grow up?"

Luca: "I like a lot of people. Judges, artists, actors, engineers, cooks and even soldiers.
When I was a kid, I liked the latter and their guns. This is the most fascinating to me. But my mother disagreed. She wanted me to become a doctor or a university professor.
I can't imagine studying for a long time, so I read something else. When I finished my studies, my first job was a librarian and then a driver, and I finally found a job as an agent."

CHINESE

罗德里戈："你的父母在哪里工作？"

卢卡："我的父亲是一名律师，我的母亲也是一名律师。"

罗德里戈："你的兄弟姐妹？"

卢卡："我的姐姐是秘书，而我的兄弟是画家。"

罗德里戈："你呢？"

卢卡："到目前为止，我已经出版了两本书，所以我可以将自己定义为作者。"

罗德里戈："你长大后想成为别的什么吗？"

卢卡："我喜欢很多人．法官、艺术家、演员、工程师、厨师甚至是士兵。

当我还是个孩子，我很喜欢后者和他们的枪。　这是最让我着迷的。但是我的母亲不同意，她想让我成为一名医生或者大学教授。

我不能想象研究很长一段时间，所以我读了些别的事情。　当我完成学业，我的第一份工作是一个图书管理员，然后一个驱动程序，和我终于找到了一份工作作为代理人。"

第13章

措施

关键词：Metro, mile, kilometers, kilograms, total.

深度	Depth
高度	Height
一公斤	One kilogram
一米	One meter
测量	Measuring
她很小，我很大	She is small, and I am very big
大象是一种巨大的动物	The elephant is a huge animal
我们用一克茶	We use one gram of tea
她有一点面包	She has a bit of bread
还剩多少厘米？	How many centimeters are left?
你做测量	You do the measurement
厘米和英寸	Centimeters and inches
我们知道的体积	We know the volume
我们有一克糖	We have one gram of sugar
在隔壁的房间里	In the next room
哪个动物很小？	Which animal is small?
我等了几个小时	I waited for a few hours
多少米？	How much rice?
我们使用公里	We use kilometers
多少公斤？	How many kilograms?
总数的四分之一	One quarter of the total
我的一半	My half
这对我来说都是一样的	This is the same for me
我们看看总数	We look at the total number

这些是双方	These are the two sides
公里	Kilometers
一英里多长时间?	How long is a mile?
我在厨房里有一升油	I have a litre of oil in the kitchen
双浓咖啡，谢谢	Double espresso, thanks
厨房里什么都没有	Nothing in the kitchen
双浓咖啡是给她的	The double espresso is for her
我的包里没有东西	There is nothing in my bag
我有一点白巧克力	I have a little white chocolate
门的宽度是八十厘米	The width of the door is 80 centimeters
深度很重要	Depth is very important
一吨有一千公斤	One ton has a thousand kilograms
你想要我的一半苹果吗?	Do you want my half apple?
八次是四次两次	Eight times is four times twice
这是一个鸡蛋的大小	This is the size of an egg
房间有正方形的形状	The room has a square shape
我们得到多少公斤肉?	How many kilograms of meat do we get?
新的速度是什么？	What is the new speed?
我的地窖里有三立方米的柴火	There are three cubic meters of firewood in my cellar
这是两卷的小说	This is a two-volume novel
正方形的边是平等的	The sides of the square are equal

我家的高度是七米 / The height of my home is seven meters

训练时间
故事模式

ENGLISH

"How fast does the engine run?" asks Prof. Makkonen, a silver hair engineer, to test his latest invention on the Eliseu Bridge.

"About nine kilometers an hour." The assistant said when he picked up a large speedometer.

"What is the height requirement for eight kilometers below sea level?"

"Four to ten feet long, sir."

"Okay, now, how does it compare to the previous one?" asked Professor Makkonen.

"This usually depends on its width and water content. At this point, the two are almost the same, from 64 pounds to 63 pounds." the assistant explained.

"Yes, but it consumes a third of its predecessor's intensity, and the total distance is greater: from 90 centimeters to two meters, instead of from 50 centimeters to one meter, so there is a difference." said the professor.

The assistant picked up the notebook and scribbled several numbers.

"Perhaps we should also increase the length by half, sir, for the purpose of aerodynamics."

"Indeed, Walter, let us work now." the professor answered.

CHINESE

"发动机工作速度有多快?"银色的头发的教授Makkonen在对他的新发明进行测试时说道。

"每小时九公里,助理说,当他拿起一个大的里程表。

海平面以下八公里的高度要求是多少?"

"长四到十英尺,先生。"

"好吧,现在,它与上一次相比有多重?"Makkonen教授问。

"这通常取决于它的宽度和含水量,在这一点上,两者几乎相同,从64磅到63磅。"助理解释说。

"是的,但它消耗了其前任的三分之一强度,而且总距离也更大:从九十厘米到两米,而不是从五十厘米到一米,所以有差别。"教授说。

助理拿起笔记本,潦草地写了几个数字。

"也许我们也应该把长度增加一半,先生,为了空气动力的目的。"

"确实,沃尔特,现在让我们工作。"教授回答。

第14章

家庭

关键词：Balcony, chair, bed, room, oven, roof, door, soap, door, curtain, desk, toothpaste, bathroom, staircase, window, apartment, wall, bathtub, light.

房子	**House**
玻璃	**Glass**
刀	**Knife**
电话	Phone
杯子	**Cup**
汤匙	Spoon
喷泉	Fountain
电视	TV
锅	Pot
沙发	**Sofa**
窗帘	**Curtain**
桌子	**Table**
门	Door
地毯	**Carpet**
办公桌	Desk
椅子	**Chair**
床	Bed
厨房	**Kitchen**
窗户	Window
光明	**Lamp**
钥匙	Key
灯	**Light**
镜子	Mirror
天花板	**Ceiling**
地上	**Above ground**

训练时间

墙	Wall
烤箱	Oven
卧室	Bedroom
洗手间	Toilet
我的枝形吊灯	My chandelier
你的刀	Your knife
我的手机很大	My phone is very big
我的汤匙是白色的	My spoon is white
我有一个浴缸	I have a bathtub
猫就在地毯上	The cat is on the carpet
我在阳台上	I am on the balcony
我们住在一个公寓里	We live in an apartment
我想要我的毯子	I want my blanket
我儿子想要一张绿色的床	My son wants a green bed
地毯是蓝色的	The carpet is blue
我的叔叔住在一间公寓里	My uncle lives in an apartment
我厨房里没有地毯	I have no carpet in my kitchen.
水很清澈	The water is very clear
你走了，我走了	You are gone, I am leaving.
我用一把椅子	I use a chair
他买了一顶帐篷	He bought a tent
今天是晴朗的一天	Today is a sunny day
猫在地毯上吃	The cat eats on the carpet
我在桌子上看书	I read a book on the table.
你打开门	You open the door

训练时间

玩具在地毯上
蛋糕在冰箱里
你的家人在桌旁
面包放在烤箱里
我妈妈在洗澡
我的母亲在厨房里
窗户是黑色的
猫在沙发上

我们在院子里等

牙膏在哪里？
床单在哪里？

我的剃刀是哪种？
你有牙刷吗？
我有一些红色的椅子

你有海绵吗？

我拿牙刷
我有一个枕头
他有一个红色电话

洛伦佐在桌旁吃饭
我们没有杯子！
卢卡睡在床上

We enter your tent
The cake is in the fridge
Where is the furniture?
We don't have heating
I am by the door
She can't find her key
The horse is at the door
The lights in the bathroom are green
They don't have furniture
They have keys
Is there a phone in the room?
Where is the shampoo?
We buy white pillows
The shampoo is in the bathroom
The red roof house is my uncle's
Where is the mirror?
I have a pillow
How many calls do you have?
Do you have a ladder?
Soap in the bathtub
I want a sofa

我有你的电视 — The kitchen is yours
在厨房 — The wall is red
一杯牛奶 — We open the window
墙壁 — The entrance is white

训练时间

玩具在地毯上 — The toy is on the carpet
为什么我们找不到儿子的玩具？ — Why can't we find the son's toy?
你的家人在桌旁 — Your family is at the table
面包放在烤箱里 — Bread in the oven
我妈妈在洗澡 — My mother is taking a shower
我的母亲在厨房里 — My mother is in the kitchen
窗户是黑色的 — The window is black
猫在沙发上 — The cat is on the couch
我们在院子里等 — We are waiting in the yard
牙膏在哪里？ — Where is the toothpaste?
床单在哪里？ — Where are the sheets?
我的剃刀是哪种？ — What kind of razor do I have?
你有牙刷吗？ — Do you have a toothbrush?
我有一些红色的椅子 — I have some red chairs
你有海绵吗？ — Do you have a sponge?
我拿牙刷 — I take a toothbrush
他的椅子 — His chair
他有一个红色电话 — He has a red phone

洛伦佐在桌旁吃饭　　　　　　　Lorenzo eats at the table

我们没有杯子！　　　　　　　　We don't have a cup!

卢卡睡在床上　　　　　　　　　Luca sleeps in bed

我有你的电视　　　　　　　　　I have your TV

在厨房　　　　　　　　　　　　In the kitchen

一杯牛奶　　　　　　　　　　　A glass of milk

墙壁　　　　　　　　　　　　　The wall

训练时间

我在卧室吃饭　　　　　　　　　I am eating in the bedroom

我没有冰箱　　　　　　　　　　I have no refrigerator

阿尔贝托清理卫生间　　　　　　Alberto cleans the bathroom

我们有一台烘干机　　　　　　　We have a dryer

那洗衣机　　　　　　　　　　　That washing machine

我没有洗衣机　　　　　　　　　I have no washing machine

习安睡在椅子上？　　　　　　　Does Xi sleep in a chair?

莫亚在烤箱里煮鸡肉　　　　　　Moya cooks chicken in the oven

他想要一台洗衣机　　　　　　　He wants a washing machine

你想要厨房用海绵吗？　　　　　Do you want a kitchen sponge?

我需要肥皂　　　　　　　　　　I need soap

雨伞不是我们的　　　　　　　　The umbrella is not ours

床单是黄色的　　　　　　　　　The sheets are yellow

我们有黄色肥皂吗？　　　　　　Do we have yellow soap?

萨拉吃肥皂！　　　　　　　　　Sarah eats soap!

剃刀是蓝色的　　　　　　　　　The razor is blue

我用水填满杯子	I fill the cup with water
颜色很自然	The color is very natural
报纸是最近的	The newspaper is the latest
我有钱	I have money
下一个小时	Next hour
茶是天然的	The tea is natural
这是一个历史性的一周	This is a historic week
谁是下一个？	Who is the next one?
报纸最近？	Is the newspaper recent?

训练时间

故事模式

ENGLISH

Jintao: "What are you doing in the wine cellar?"

Fang: "I am looking for my mobile phone."

Jintao: "Have you checked behind this wall? I saw you standing by the window some time ago."

Fang: "I check everywhere, inside the washing machine, the table is everywhere."

Jintao: "Where did you see it last time?"

Fang: "On the sheets folded in my room."

Jintao: "Try to remember your way."

Fang: "Well, when my dad called, I was cleaning the bathroom mirror. When the call ended, I changed the light from the ceiling of the room, then I remembered the rain. I needed to clean the pool, so I opened the closet and took an umbrella. And some soap.
After that, I went back to the kitchen and opened the fridge to drink juice. I put my phone close to the cup and some dishes. There is also a knife on the kitchen table. I went back to the room, where I decided to take a drink before I took a nap. This is what I remember."

Jintao: "Let's go back to the bedroom."

CHINESE

金涛："你在酒窖里干什么？"

方："我正在寻找我的手机。"

金涛："你在这堵墙后面检查过吗？我前段时间看到你站在窗边。"

方："我到处检查，洗衣机里面，桌子上到处都是。"

金涛："你上次在哪里看到它？"

方："在我房间折叠的床单上面。"

金涛："试着记住你的方式。"

方："嗯，当我爸爸打电话，我是打扫浴室镜子。当电话结束时，我从房间的天花板上改变了光线，然后我想起了雨。 **我需要清理游泳池，所以我打开衣柜拿了一把**伞和一些肥皂。

之后，我回到厨房，打开冰箱喝果汁。我把我的手机靠近杯子和一些菜。厨房的桌子上还有一把刀。我回到房间，在那里我决定打个盹之前喝了一杯果汁。这就是我记得的"

金涛："让我们回到卧室。"

第15章

形容词

关键词：Strong, full, common, free, strange, long.

再次？	Once again?
最后	At last
我感冒了	I am sick
它不一样	It is different
这个女人很漂亮	This woman is very beautiful
她不老	She is not old
这是可能的	This is possible
他们的制服是新的	Their uniform is new
他的答案与我的不同	His answer is different from mine.
这是相同的	This is the same
他要的是不可能的	What he wants is impossible
当个好姑娘！	Be a good girl!
全国颜色为绿色和黄色	The national colors are green and yellow
他们高吗？	Are they tall?
这是一个很好的蛋糕	This is a good cake
我很矮	I am short
我们不是国际性的	We are not international
它并不昂贵	It is not expensive
我姐姐很有名	My sister is very famous
作家并不出名	The writer is not famous
我们的牙膏很便宜	Our toothpaste is very cheap
这个包是免费的	This package is free

我今天有空	I am free today.
我知道你很富有	I know that you are very rich.
你有外国啤酒吗？	Do you have foreign beer?

训练时间

这是我的日常面包	This is my daily bread
她是一位现代母亲	She is a modern mother
我有一个电烤架	I have an electric grill
她很受欢迎	She is very popular
对他来说重要的是什么？	What is important to him?
这匹马是一种有用的动物	This horse is a useful animal
这是一个悬而未决的问题	This is an open question
你感兴趣吗？	Are you interested?
我们完美吗？	Are we perfect?
你是唯一的孩子吗？	Are you the only child?
我有能力	I am capable
红苹果并不特别	The red apple is not special
他有一件有趣的服装	He has an interesting costume
你表弟的工作很有意思	Your cousin's work is very interesting.
你保持窗户关闭	You keep the window closed
你不是唯一的一个	You are not the only one
她很坚强	She is very strong
我们并不难	We are not difficult

蘑菇汤有一种奇怪的味道	Mushroom soup has a strange taste
我的祖母一个人住	My grandmother lives alone.
鲨鱼很危险	Sharks are dangerous
我的儿子很大	My son is very big
我带上厚重的靴子	I bring heavy boots
夜晚很长	Very long night
下一杯咖啡是你的	The next cup of coffee is yours

训练时间

对她来说很容易	Easy for her
我吃饱了	I'm stuffed
我吃了一整只鸡	I ate a whole chicken.
她对他们很强硬	She is very tough on them
我的短裙是白色和蓝色	My skirt is white and blue
这是一份普通的报纸	This is an ordinary newspaper
这是真的	This is real
早**餐**准备好了	Breakfast is ready
我确定	I am sure
你的答案是对的	Your answer is correct.
他是一个普通人	He is an ordinary person
我们决定，因为我们确定	We decided because we determined
你的答案不明确	Your answer is not clear
我们的时间很短暂	Our time is short
汤变冷了	The soup is getting cold

她很年轻，我老了	She is very young, I am old.
今天天气好热	The weather is hot today.
二月是短暂的一个月	February is a short month
他们有热三明治吗？	Do they have hot sandwiches?
她的问题很难	Her problem is difficult
他是一名优秀的学生	He is an excellent student
她睡在空荡荡的房间里	She slept in an empty room
窗帘很脏	The curtains are dirty
一份文化报纸	A cultural newspaper
他很强壮	He is very strong

训练时间

我们是人	We are people
厨房不安全	The kitchen is not safe
我们高大强壮	We are tall and strong
我有足够的衣服	I have enough clothes
他更糟糕	He is even worse
我需要干衣服	I need to dry clothes
这很容易	This is easy
请一些果汁	Please, some juice
他讲得很快	He spoke very quickly
我不是外国人	I am not a foreigner
毯子很薄	The blanket is very thin
他们的书很少	Their books are rare
他是一个言辞不多的人	He is a person with few words

窗帘很薄	The curtains are very thin
我的女儿喜欢薄意大利面	My daughter likes thin spaghetti
我的书很少	Very few books
我们喝得很快	We drink very quickly
地板很脏	The floor is dirty
她的洗发水很贵	Her shampoo is expensive
我们并不难	We are not difficult
他有空口袋	He has empty pockets
我们有一个空置的房间	We have a vacant room
不，这很简单	No, this is simple
我认为这是不可能的	I think this is impossible.
我读了一份全国性报纸	I read a national newspaper.

训练时间

他是一名工业化学家	He is an industrial chemist
这不是司空见惯的事	This is not a common thing.
国家的颜色是红色，黑色和黄色	The colors of the country are red, black and yellow
她的厨房是工业用的	Her kitchen is industrial
是的，很简单	Yes, it's very simple
他们很穷	They are very poor
她很坦率	She is very frank
什么是历史时期？	What is the historical period?
柠檬水很自然	Lemonade is very natural

他们不负责任	They are not responsible
墙是永久的	The wall is permanent
因为我是个坏人	Because I am a bad person
我穷	I am poor
这是一个历史性的一周	This is a historic week
它们不自然	They are not natural
坦率地说	Frankly speaking
我们不负责任	We are not responsible
果汁是天然的	Juice is natural
他很穷	He is very poor
我有一只漂亮的鸭子	I have a beautiful duck
他们是好学生	They are good students
他们吃同一盘子	They eat the same plate
你做得很好	You did very well
你是双语的	You are bilingual
这件衣服漂亮	This dress is beautiful

训练时间

他们是年轻人	They are young people
她有同样的杯子	She has the same cup
她是一位老法官	She is an old judge
好问题	good question
同样的汤	The same soup
苹果很好	The apple is very good
有用吗？	Is that useful?
这是一本新书	This is a new book
你比我好	You are better than me
灯很难看	The lights are hard to see

我的弟弟	My brother
我比我妹妹大	I am bigger than my sister.
不，你是第一个	No, you are the first
我们不是新人	We are not new people
我们有最好的	We have the best
我们是年长的兄弟姐妹	We are older brothers and sisters
他难看吗？	Is he ugly?
你想要新衣服吗？	Do you want new clothes?
是的，它是真实的	Yes, it is real
你是一个积极的人	You are an active person
我们是最后一个	We are the last one
是的，他们是真的	Yes, they are real
这不可能	This is impossible
是的，这很重要	Yes, this is very important
这是最后一刻	This is the last moment

训练时间

你不是真的！	You are not real!
我的兄弟很重要	My brother is very important
他是一个积极的老板	He is an active boss
昨晚很漫长	It was very long last night.
明天是我的最后一天	Tomorrow is my last day
很难	Hard
鞋是必要的	Shoes are necessary
这是一个公共党派	This is a public party
作者独自行走	The author walks alone

你很受孩子们的欢迎	You are very popular with children.
你和我是不同的	You are different from me.
这是我的私人电话	This is my private phone
他一个人走路	He walks by himself
公共浴室	Public bath
我们不受欢迎	We are not welcome
不，他们没有必要	No, they are not necessary
盘子很硬	The plate is very hard
他们是公共工作者	They are public workers
我们高大强壮	We are tall and strong
主要颜色	Primary color
他是一个能干的人	He is a capable person
动物是独特的	Animals are unique
我看当地电视台	I watch the local TV station.
这很安全	This is safe
大门	Door

训练时间

她是一个坚强的人	She is a strong person
我们是不同的	We are different
她是你唯一的妹妹	She is your only sister
那还不够	That is not enough
接下来的几周	The next few weeks
他是一名职业演员	He is a professional actor
我自己的儿子	My own son
她比我差	She is worse than me
什么是不可能的？	What is impossible?

这件衣服很简单	This dress is very simple
我有自己的狗	I have my own dog
我们不是专业演员	We are not professional actors
他们有自己的派对	They have their own party
他是坏人	He is a bad person
我很正常	I am normal
他们不负责任	They are not responsible
我读的书不多	I don't read many books.

训练时间

故事模式

ENGLISH

"Alvaro let's play a game called 'objective statements.' The goal of the game is to make a statement using the word 'but' in five seconds, or drink from this bottle. I will start."

"He's sick, but the room is clean."

Zhu: "The book is strange but special."

Alvaro: "The bottle is big, but the price is regular."

Zhu: "It's old, but it's free to download."

Alvaro: "The powder is dark, but pure."

Zhu: "Five is the minimum, but I have four."

Alvaro: "The maps are similar, but I'm lost."

Zhu: "These shoes are good but not original."

Alvaro: "These bags are classic, but not superior."

Zhu: "The car is dirty, but it's perfect."

Alvaro: "It's brilliant, but not famous."

Zhu: "It's more difficult, but convenient."

Alvaro: "My boyfriend is sweet but also terrible. "

CHINESE

"阿尔瓦罗,让我们玩一个叫做'**客观陈述**'的游戏。游戏的目标是在五秒内使用'**但是**'这个词做出声明,或者从这个瓶子里喝水。 我会开始的。"

"他生病了,**但房**间很干净。"

朱:"这本书很奇怪但很特别。"

阿尔瓦罗:"瓶子很大,但价格很高。"

朱:"它已经老了,但可以免费下载。"

阿尔瓦罗:"粉末很黑,但很纯净。"

朱:"五是最小的,但我有四个。"

阿尔瓦罗:"地图很相似,但我输了。"

朱:"这些鞋子好但不是原创的。"

阿尔瓦罗:"这些包包很经典,但并不优越。"

朱:"汽车很脏,但很完美。"

阿尔瓦罗:"这很棒,但并不出名。"

朱:"这更难,但更方便。"

阿尔瓦罗:"我男朋友很甜,也很可怕。"

第16章

限定词

关键词：These, too, this, certain, all, other, each.

新的	New
工作	Jobs
活动	The activity
可能性	The possibility
她有太多的猫	She has too many cats
所有的女人都在这里	All the women are here
蜜蜂不是蝴蝶	The bee is not a butterfly
这本书太贵了	This book is too expensive
这茶很好吃	This tea is delicious
我们有一面红镜	We have a red mirror
这些包是红色的	These bags are red
这种胡萝卜很甜	This carrot is very sweet
这些书是新的	These books are new
这辆汽车就像新车一样	This car is like a new car
这两位管道工是堂兄弟	These two plumbers are cousins.
那个人不是我的丈夫	That person is not my husband
她不适合那辆车	She is not suitable for that car
那座城堡是白色的	The castle is white
你知道那家酒店吗？	Do you know that hotel?
我认识那些女人	I know those women
整个村庄做饭	Cooking in the entire village
她整夜工作	She works all night
我有很多油	I have a lot of oil

我没有朋友	I do not have friends
这里有很多人	There are many people here.

训练时间

你记得那些年了吗？	Do you remember those years?
他每天早上都喝一瓶牛奶	He drinks a bottle of milk every morning.
我读过几份报纸	I have read several newspapers.
我不喜欢那些手机	I don't like those phones.
那些衬衫对他来说太小了	Those shirts are too small for him.
房间里有几件衬衫	There are a few shirts in the room.
公园里有几个男生	There are several boys in the park.
每天都有各种女性打电话	Every day, every woman calls
动物园里有各种各样的动物	There are all kinds of animals in the zoo.
我不想为我的婚礼举办派对	I don't want to have a party for my wedding.
服务员在另一个酒吧工作	The waiter works in another bar
某些事情随着时间而变化	Some things change over time
某些人不像他一样工作	Some people don't work like him
你知道一些好的商店吗？	Do you know some good stores?
我不和某些人合作	I don't work with some people.
太多事情都不清楚	Too many things are not clear
他喝了太多酒	He drank too much wine

他喝了太多啤酒	He drank too much beer
某些人不吃蔬菜	Some people don't eat vegetables
我们知道很多事情	We know a lot of things
公园里人太多了	There are too many people in the park.
有些女人更漂亮	Some women are more beautiful
我们在动物园看到了所有的动物	We saw all the animals at the zoo.
我们有几百万	We have millions
整个家庭都在农场工作	The entire family works on the farm
我想要任何一种蔬菜	I want any kind of vegetables
任何座位都可以	Any seat can be
你知道，我没有任何家庭	You know, I don't have any family.
他们有另一个儿子	They have another son
我爱他和我的全家	I love him and my family.
你想要另一杯茶吗？	Do you want another cup of tea?
这些苹果很大	These apples are very big
有些女人喝绿茶	Some women drink green tea
那些男人为什么看着你？	Why are those men looking at you?
我更喜欢那个黑色的	I prefer that black one.
谁的眼镜是这些？	Whose glasses are these?
她有太多的男朋友	She has too many boyfriends
我有另一个女儿，但她更大	I have another daughter, but she is bigger
我想要另一种啤酒	I want another beer

训练时间

故事模式

ENGLISH

Wei Wei: "How many windows are there in this house? Everyone says eight years old, but I don't agree."

Shen: "My bathroom has no windows, so there are seven."

Wei Wei: "And the house in Valencia? How much?"

Shen: "Four."

Wei Wei: "Four? Considering the size of the room, you need a lot of ventilation."

Shen: "Some windows are expensive, and it is difficult to buy more than 7."

Wei Wei: "If you have your own mobile phone, you should check some pictures on my website. The price of each picture is less than $70. I think they can be accessed, and the quality is the same as other brands."

* searches online*

Shen: "The windows are beautiful, especially the two in the upper left corner. I like these two."

Wei Wei: "I know you will like it, because I hope that you can be my first customer this month. If you can afford it, I can offer a 5% discount."

Shen: "Yes, I can, can I take your phone number?"

CHINESE

薇薇："这个房子里有多少个窗户？每个人都说八岁，但我不同意。"

沉："我的浴室没有窗户，所以有七个。"

薇薇："和在瓦伦西亚的房子？多少?"

沉："四。"

薇薇："四个？考虑到房间的大小，你需要大量的通风。"

沉："有些窗户价格昂贵，很难购买超过7个。"

薇薇："如果你有自己的手机，你应该查看我网站上的一些图片。每张图片的价格都不到70美元。我认为它们可以访问，质量与其他品牌相同。"

在网上找

沉："窗户很漂亮，特别是左上角的两个。我喜欢这两个。"

薇薇："我知道你会喜欢它，因为我希望你能成为我这个月的第一个顾客。如果你买得起，我可以提供5%的折扣。"

沉："是的，我可以，我可以拿你的电话号码吗？"

第17章

副词

关键词：Much, little, much, above, below.

好的	Ok
几乎	Almost
他吃了很多东西	He ate a lot of things
你是如此强大	You are so powerful
他们从哪里来？	Where are they from?
这非常贵	This is very expensive
我知道他来自哪里	I know where he is from
你的包有多重？	How many bags do you have?
你是从那里来的吗？	Are you from there?
它不是很贵	It is not very expensive
这周我工作很多	I work a lot this week.
他们住在那里	They live there
我们对他知之甚少	We know very little about him.
蜘蛛在奶酪下面	The spider is under the cheese
这只鸟在动物园上面	This bird is above the zoo
我们在餐厅外面	We are outside the restaurant
十多年了	More than ten years
我在外面等	I am waiting outside
春天来了	spring is coming
他们和她一起进去	They went in with her
她环顾四周	She looks around
我晚饭后出去	I go out after dinner.
然后女人们到了	Then the women are here.

你在这里和我们在一起接着？	You are here with us then?

训练时间

我也是	Me too
我想要的时候吃	I eat when I want
星期六在星期日之前到来	Saturday comes before Sunday
你尽可能多地吃	You eat as much as possible
邮递员的公寓在这里	The postman's apartment is here
你经常给父母写信吗？	Do you often write letters to your parents?
冬天过后春天来临	Spring is coming after winter
你妹妹一如既往地美丽	Your sister is as beautiful as ever
我的母亲更好	My mother is better
好的，谢谢	Okay thank you
真的对不起	Really sorry
谢谢，他们很好	Thank you, they are very good
我哥哥从不喝酒	My brother never drinks
我很好	I'm very good
去你想去的任何地方	Go anywhere you want
不太甜蜜	Not too sweet
他们也来了吗？	Are they here too?
几乎是中午	Almost noon
你一个人吗？	Are you alone?
我不吃太多	I don't eat too much
我马上到了	I am here soon.
我不太确定	I am not sure
他们也住在这里	They also live here

显然，水果很甜	Obviously, the fruit is very sweet
那他们为什么在这里？	Then why are they here?

训练时间

水管工还在吗？	Is the plumber still there?
这绝对不可能	This is absolutely impossible
他还在这里	He is still here
它完全是绿色的	It is completely green
及时	Timely
这匹马还很年轻	This horse is still very young
到处都是这样的	Everywhere is like this
我们已经六月了	We are already in June
你有孩子吗？	Do you have children?
这很有意思	This is very interesting
但日期并不确定	But the date is not certain
至少他们在餐桌旁吃饭	At least they are eating at the table
我不吃肉，但我吃鱼	I don't eat meat, but I eat fish.
无论如何，这并不重要	In any case, this is not important
已经是周五了吗？	Already Friday?
有一只猫	Have a cat
你就像你的母亲	You are like your mother
我们现在要走了	We are leaving now
为什么我们连一个叉子都没有？	Why don't we even have a fork?

我每年写一本书	I write a book every year.
我们一起去吗？	Let's go together?
桌子上有一个苹果	There is an apple on the table
它只是一只老鼠	It's just a mouse
我主要讲他们	I mainly talk about them.
今天，我确定	Today, I am sure

训练时间

非常远	Very far
通常	Usually
不，目前没有	No, not yet
终于来了	Finally
回头见	See you later
再见	Goodbye
当然，真的是他	Of course, it is really him.
我确定答案	I am sure
也许三月，但不是四月	Maybe March, but not April
也许它是巧克力饼干	Maybe it's chocolate chip cookies
也许她会做晚饭	Maybe she will cook dinner
也许这是真的	Maybe this is true
她在那	She is there
一般来说，它是白色的	Generally, it is white
你特别为我们写	You write for us specifically
最后，是星期五	Finally, it is Friday.
你睡了很多吗？	Have you slept a lot?
你很漂亮	You are very beautiful
我妹妹从不喝酒	My sister never drinks

这完全正常	This is completely normal
我只有一双鞋	I only have a pair of shoes
她走来走去	She is walking around
他讲得很好	He spoke very well
我哥哥从不喝酒	My brother never drinks
这完全不同！	This is totally different!

训练时间

全然	Completely
无疑	Undoubtedly
究竟！	Exactly!
我从不游泳	I never swim
你真的是个好人	You are really a good person.
是的，我立即去	Yes, I will go immediately
也许这太过分了	Maybe this is too much
同样，再见	Again, goodbye
他可能今天到了	He may have arrived today.
在桌子下面	Under the table
我们继续前进	We move on
你几乎是我的兄弟	You are almost my brother
同样，谢谢你，医生	Again, thank you, doctor
也许这是可能的	Maybe this is possible
我的猫睡在沙发下面	My cat is sleeping under the sofa

猪在桌子下面	The pig is under the table
他们同样负责任	They are equally responsible
他们马上到达	They arrive right away
他只吃意大利面	He only eats pasta
这是完全可能的	This is entirely possible
她主要吃糖	She mainly eats sugar
他又一个人了	He is another person
是的，最近	Yes, recently
它完全是绿色的	It is completely green
她只吃水果	She only eats fruit

训练时间

我们在这里	We are here
它主要是糖	It is mainly sugar
你完全有能力	You are fully capable
我们最近谈过	We have talked recently
年轻，自然	Young, natural
我们喝的很快	We drink very quickly
这肯定是我的大象	This must be my elephant
一匹马跑得很快	A horse runs very fast
它们究竟是什么？	What exactly are they?
我绝对肯定	I am absolutely sure
是的，你肯定更好	Yes, you are definitely better.
当然是果汁	Juice, of course
星期三，通常	Wednesday, usually
他走得很慢	He walks very slowly
不必要	Unnecessary
她很容易读	She is easy to read
可能更糟糕	May be worse

他的儿子几乎不说话	His son barely speaks
这是相对较新的	This is relatively new
他慢慢吃	He eats slowly
通常，需要数年时间	Usually, it takes years
过去一周	The past week
冰箱很便宜	The refrigerator is very cheap
你几乎不是男孩	You're hardly a boy
它不一定是一个人	It is not necessarily a person

训练时间

故事模式

ENGLISH

"Finally, will you come to the club on Friday?" said Nicole. "Possibly." Shen replied.

"If you don't go in, you will miss it. There will be drinks and celebrities."

"It all depends on my sister. If she leaves, I will leave. Before that, I have not decided yet." Shen replied.

"You have to decide now; the VIP part is one of the best parts of the world." Nicole continued.

"I am still hesitating." Shen said.

"If you finally change your mind, it may be too late, and you will never have the chance to see your favorite artist again." said Nicole.

CHINESE

"最后,你星期五会来俱乐部吗?"尼可说。

"可能,"沉回答道。

"如果你不进去,你会错过。会有饮料和名人。"

"这完全取决于我的妹妹。如果她离开,我会离开。在那之前,我还没有决定,"沉回答道。

"你现在必须决定;VIP部分是世界上最好的部分之一。"尼可说继续说道。

"我还在犹豫,"沉说。

"如果你最终改变主意,可能为时已晚,你再也没有机会再看到你最喜欢的艺术家了,"尼可说。

第18章

物体

关键词：Car, machine, box, comb, wheel, ball, glasses.

电机	Motor
笔	Pen
地图	Map
瓶子	Bottle
电脑	Computer
火车	Train
自行车	Bicycle
球	Ball
钥匙	Key
一辆车	A car
一块	The piece
收音机	Radio
那个飞机	That plane
相机	Camera
电池	Battery
背包	Backpack
剪刀	Scissors
卡片	Card
这艘船	This ship
脚	Foot
我想要很多东西	I want a lot of things
这是件老事	This is an old thing
我有车	I have a car
硬币很大	Big coin
我的手机	My cell phone

训练时间

关键	The key
钱	Money
该杂志	The magazine
报纸	Newspaper
钟声	The bell
杯子	Cup
头脑	Mind
这座桥	The bridge
黄金	Gold
链	Chain
论文	Paper
美元	The dollar
这些事	These things
电影	The film
该文件	The document
手机	Mobile phone
屏幕	Screen
你养日记吗？	Do you keep a diary?
你还有刷吗？	Do you still have a brush?
我也有日记	I also have a diary.
他们有电脑吗？	Do they have a computer?
女孩的梳子	The girl's comb
我已经有了一个信封	I already have an envelope
盒子放在桌子上	The box is placed on the table

| 我们有一盒饼干 | We have a box of cookies |

训练时间

硬币	Coin
国旗	Flag
账单	Bill
汽车	Car
车轮	Wheel
武器	Arms
刷子	Brush
信封	Envelope
梳子	Comb
日记	Diary
照片	Photo
武器	The arms
图片	The image
叶子	Leaf
他想要一些红色眼镜	He wants some red glasses
我们夏天有新粉丝	We have new fans in the summer.
他身体状况很好	He is in good health
我有完美的礼物	I have the perfect gift
这是一小块	This is a small piece
我看到一个键盘	I saw a keyboard
今天，我拿到了执照	Today, I got the license.
我想要礼物	I want a gift
我找不到我的执照	I can't find my license.
我父亲有长笛和小提琴	My father has a flute and a violin.

她总是说同样的话　　She always said the same thing

训练时间

引擎	Engine
酒精	Alcohol
手提包	Handbag
我们的瓶子	Our bottle
边缘	The edge
黄金是我的！	The gold is mine!
我写在白纸上	I am writing on white paper
我有一个轮子和一个引擎	I have a wheel and an engine
你永远没有时间去做重要的事情	You never have time to do important things
这是一张白纸	This is a blank sheet of paper
汽车没油了	The car is out of oil
我想为我的车买一块电池	I want to buy a battery for my car.
谁有这个乐器？	Who has this instrument?
这艘船很旧	This ship is very old
我堂兄的汽车很新	My cousin's car is very new.
我们有车	We have a car
船长说的是船	The captain is talking about the ship.
这是我的车	This is my car
我有一个代码	I have a code

你是机器吗？	Are you a machine?
这是一个专栏	This is a column
我们现在读报纸	We read the newspaper now
他总是读一本杂志	He always reads a magazine
这个女孩写了很多页	This girl wrote a lot of pages
她需要冰箱的一部分	She needs a part of the refrigerator

训练时间

电池	The battery
她有一个连锁店	She has a chain store
她有一对蓝眼睛	She has a pair of blue eyes
我们看报纸	We read the newspaper
碗里的物体是什么？	What is the object in the bowl?
她的衣服是独一无二的	Her clothes are unique
这总是一件好事	This is always a good thing
他有一点点钱	He has a little money
她有纸吗？	Does she have paper?
我有一个球	I have a ball
我有车	I have a car
胡里奥把黄油涂在脚上	Julio puts butter on his feet
我的行李箱是黄色的	My suitcase is yellow
我有文字	I have text
电视很贵	TV is expensive
手表是一个对象	The watch is an object
他下午喝酒	He drinks in the afternoon

他把钱给了男人们	He gave the money to the men
猫睡在狗的上面	The cat sleeps on the top of the dog
他生产昂贵的物品	He produces expensive items
他们付了一美元	They paid a dollar
狗粮很贵	Dog food is expensive
你有手机吗？	Do you have a cell phone?
我姐姐的行李箱很大	My sister's suitcase is very big.
你有硬币吗？	Do you have a coin?

训练时间

照片	Photo
屏幕	Screen
眼	Eye
头部	Head
国旗	Flag
消息来源	Source
引擎	Engine
武器	Arms
车轮	Wheel
粉末	Powder
机器	Machine
碎片	Fragment
盒子	Box
瓶子	Bottle
我需要电池	I need a battery
我不喜欢那件事	I don't like that thing.
律师发表论文	The lawyer published a paper
谁有文件？	Who has the file?
还有谁在船上？	Who else is on board?

你有相机吗？	Do you have a camera?
我的船是蓝色的	My boat is blue
你有手表吗？	Do you have a watch?
报纸是最近的	The newspaper is recent
该文件有很多页面	This file has many pages
我想要一份奶酪三明治和一杯水	I want a cheese sandwich and a glass of water.

训练时间

和平	Peace
该部门	Department
运动	Movement
这个调查	This survey
容量	Capacity
必要性	Necessity
效果	Effect
代码	Code
我用卡付款	I pay by card
这是钱的来源	This is the source of money
你有笔吗？	Do you have a pen?
这是钟声	This is the bell
一个大的对象	A large object
它不是时钟	It is not a clock
我需要英文杂志	I need an English magazine.

个人物品	**Personal items**
这是美元	This is the dollar
这是我的车	This is my car
他乘公共汽车去上班吗？	Does he go to work by bus?
我们有自行车	We have bicycles
上校有一枚炸弹	The colonel has a bomb
我有笔	I have a pen
显示器很大	Large display
这是一个带笔记的瓶子	This is a bottle with notes
啤酒是给农民的	Beer is for farmers

训练时间

武器	The arms
脊椎	The spine
你是机器吗？	Are you a machine?
她**遵守**规则	She obeys the rules
她很聪明	She is very smart
作者读到了电机	The author has read the motor
这是件坏事	This is a bad thing
轮子是白色的	The wheels are white
炸弹很糟糕	The bomb is terrible
他有车	He has a car
哪款鞋适合你？	Which shoe is right for you?
她给你看了一份报纸	She showed you a newspaper

以后我会来看你	I will come to see you later.
他跟着我	He followed me
我要你	I want you
你吃了一个苹果	You ate an apple
这些鞋子不适合我	These shoes are not for me.
你跟着我	You follow me
他看着你	He looks at you
我们吃了一个橘子	We ate an orange
你跟他们说话	You talk to them
他们很聪明，不是吗？	They are smart, aren't they?
我的鞋很贵	My shoes are expensive
她责备我们	She blames us
灯很贵	The lamp is expensive

训练时间

故事模式

ENGLISH

Guangyi: "Today we will learn about objects from the pictures on the board. From left to right, each of you will name seven objects on the board and discuss their use.

Zeng! Let's start with you. Please start."

Zeng: "Apple, ball, battery, bicycle, clock, bottle, box."

Fanzhi: "calendar, camera, car, mobile phone, clock, computer, mug."

Kim: "Dollars, flags, houses, keys, maps, paper, pens."

Li: "Image, radio, scissors, boat, suitcase, train, wheels."

CHINESE

广义:"今天我们将从板上的图片中了解物体。从左到右,你们每个人都会在板上命名七个物体并继续讨论它们的用途。

曾!让我们从你开始吧。请开始。"

曾:"苹果,球,电池,自行车,钟,瓶,盒。"

梵志:"日历,相机,汽车,手机,时钟,电脑,马克杯。"

金:"美元,旗帜,房屋,钥匙,地图,纸张,钢笔。"

李:"图像,收音机,剪刀,船,手提箱,火车,轮子。"

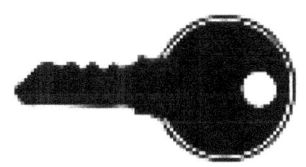

第19章

地点

关键词：Province, bookstore, theater, confectionery, palace, bridge, corner, park, supermarket, place, prison, field, station, square, street, hotel, country, museum.

酒店	Hotel
餐厅	Restaurant
家	Family
学校	School
图书馆	Library
飞机场	The airport
坐骑	The mountain
网站	Website
这座桥	The bridge
角落	Corner
中心	Center
场	Field
银行	Bank
教堂	Church
城堡	Castle
市场	Market
广场	The square
该区域	This area
剧院	Theater
酒吧	The bar
院子	Courtyard
区	The area
办公室	The office
建筑物	The building

训练时间

监狱	Prison
公园	Park
博物馆	Museum
小岛	Small island
花园	Garden
自治市	Municipality
大道	Avenue
休息室	Lounge
住所	Residence
咖啡	Coffee
小镇	Small town
马路	Road
沙滩	Beach
首都	Capital
法庭	Court
我看到城堡了	I saw the castle.
我们在同一家酒店吗？	Are we at the same hotel?
谁进入书店日？	Who entered the bookstore?
我们的面包店很小	Our bakery is small
建筑物是巨大的	The building is huge
她从面包店买面包	She buys bread from the bakery
书店在哪？	Where is the bookstore?
哪家书店出售他的书？	Which bookstore sells his book?
新建筑非常庞大	The new building is very large
从屋顶，我们看到了城堡	From the roof we saw the castle

训练时间

我爸爸有个酒吧	My father has a bar
这是一座山上的城市	This is a mountain city
这个家庭在田野里工作	This family works in the fields
晚上，我们去拐角处的酒吧	In the evening, we went to the bar at the corner
我很了解这座城市	I know the city very well
她在田野里奔跑	She is running in the field
厨房位于住宅的中心	The kitchen is in the center of the house
我们住在一个大的地区	We live in a large area
我的位置在哪里？	Where is my location?
你看到公园的入口吗？	Do you see the entrance to the park?
你想要哪个地方？	Which place do you want?
我去了你的地方	I went to your place
他们在体育场	They are at the stadium
整个地区	The entire area
国际社会的名称是什么？	What is the name of the international community?
新超市就在这里	The new supermarket is here
明天，我去村里	Tomorrow, I am going to the village
剧院很大	The theater is very big
哪条街通往这座城市？	Which street leads to the city?
这些城镇不同	These towns are different

我去一条街	I am going to a street
我们从车站到达	We arrived from the station
他在一家商店工作	He works in a store

训练时间

广场	The square
卧室	Bedroom
港口	Port
小岛	Small island
附近	Nearby
该省	The province
塔	Tower
家	Family
马路	Road
图书馆	The library
体育场	Stadium
广场	Street
街头	Theater
剧院	Station
车站	City
城市	We live in the mountains of the neighbors
我们住在山上的邻居	He has an old train conductor uniform
他有一个旧的火车售票员制服	We saw the palace tonight
我们今晚看到了宫殿	The neighboring women are very beautiful
邻里妇女很漂亮	Today, we are eating in the palace
今天，我们在宫殿里吃饭	Party near my home

派对在我家附近 — He lives in an important palace

他住在一个重要的宫殿里 — It is the city of the church

它是教会的城市 — Zhu eats at the restaurant

朱在餐厅吃饭 — He wants land

训练时间

殖民地	Colony
画廊	Gallery
大陆	The mainland
他访问了该机构	He visited the institution
这是我的地区	This is my area
欢迎来到我的餐厅	Welcome to my restaurant
欢迎来到酒店	Welcome to the hotel
徐在海滩散步	Xu walks on the beach
安娜在院子里	Anna is in the yard
朱在花园里	Zhu in the garden
去天安门广场的火车在哪里？	Where is the train to Tiananmen Square?
我在每个国家都有一所房子	I have a house in every country
这个地方似乎很大	This place seems very big
这是他的区域	This is his area
我在这个城市	I am in this city
我的房子没有屋顶	My house has no roof
城市并不好	The city is not good
这些地方很小	These places are small
建筑很大	Great building
安娜在公园里玩	Anna plays in the park

博物馆在哪里？	Where is the museum?
这是一条重要的途径	This is an important way
非洲不是一个国家	Africa is not a country
我们走在广场上	We walked on the square
广场很大很漂亮	The square is very beautiful

训练时间

国家	Country
这些地区	These areas
地形	Terrain
我的叔叔在意大利有一所房子	My uncle has a house in Italy.
社区说英语	The community speaks English
她去了大学	She went to college
她对银行了解很多	She knows a lot about the bank.
我们谈到了这些地区	We talked about these areas
我们是一个庞大的社区	We are a huge community
我们走在路边	We are walking on the side of the road
银行是白人	The bank is white
这是一个很好的医院	This is a very good hospital
在海岸	On the coast
这是一个重要的港口	This is an important port
我妹妹去了研究所	My sister went to the institute.

它是该国最好的机构	It is the best institution in the country
这些房间非常宽敞	These rooms are very spacious
这些机构依靠我们	These institutions rely on us
这是一个很大的领土	This is a big territory
你的**房子**是宫殿	Your house is a palace

训练时间

故事模式

ENGLISH

Angelo: "Before I go home, I need a new place to relax. Do you have any suggestions?"

Anna: "This is not a problem. There are many places in the city, some of which include museums, art galleries, state libraries, shopping centers and many bars and restaurants. If you like nature, you can go to the national park."

Angelo: "Where is it?"

Anna: "It's just around the cooking school and airport in the sixth district. A few blocks west of the university gate and hospital building."

Angelo: "I need a place close to my home. This distance is too far for me."

Anna: "Or, you can visit El Maria Castle. It is in a quiet area not far from the office, or even the Torre de Santa Maria owned by the Santa Maria family. It also has a bar and a small private beach."

Angelo: "How do I get there?"

Anna: "It is close to Oswald Boulevard, the second street behind the Urban Development Institute."

CHINESE

安杰洛："在我回家之前,我需要一个新的地方放松。你有什么建议吗?"

安娜："这不是问题。这个城市有很多地方,其中一些包括博物馆,艺术画廊,州立图书馆,购物中心和许多酒吧和餐馆。

如果你喜欢大自然,你可以去国家公园。"

安杰洛："它在哪里?"

安娜："它就在第六区的烹饪学校和机场附近。在大学门和医院大楼以西几个**街区**。"

安杰洛："我需要一个靠近我家的地方。这个距离对我来说太远了。"

安娜："或者,您可以参观El Maria城堡。它位于离办公室不远的一个安静的区域,甚至是Santa Maria家族拥有的Torre de Santa Maria。它还有一个酒吧和一个小型私人海滩。"

安杰洛："我怎么去那里?"

安娜："它靠近奥斯瓦尔德大道,这是城市发展研究所背后的第二条街。"

第20章

人

关键词：Adult, children, humans, people, person.

人民	People
这位女士	This lady
皇后	Queen
那个公民	The citizen
邻居	Neighbor
幼稚	Naive
受害者	Victim
囚犯	Prisoner
个人	Personal
同事	Colleague
我们有一群朋友	We have a group of friends
我们给成年人和孩子们什么？	What do we give to adults and children?
我爱我的未婚夫	I love my fiance
他们年龄相同	They are the same age
我家里的孩子都很高大	My children are very tall at home.
人群等待答案	The crowd waits for the answer
我们是个人	We are individuals
你现在是个成年人	You are an adult now.
下一杯咖啡是你的	The next cup of coffee is yours
我不是客人	I am not a guest
他是我的伙伴	He is my partner
警察搜寻一个危险的人	The police search for a dangerous person
下周将举行着名的婚礼	A famous wedding will be held next week.

我们是下一个	We are next
工会很大	The union is very big

训练时间

我的儿子只是一个少年	My son is just a teenager
这个城市的人口很多	The city has a large population
谁是下一个？	Who is next?
我是小孩	I am a child
她不是我的未婚妻！	She is not my fiancee!
人们怎么想？	What do people think?
市民听取他的答案	The public listened to his answer
新一代了解	A new generation of understanding
我不是一个普通人	I am not an ordinary person
她性格坚强	She is strong in character
先生们女士们晚上好	Good night, gentlemen and ladies.
他的父亲遇见了新娘	His father met the bride
我们不是同事	We are not colleagues
我们不是公民	We are not citizens
我和姨妈有特殊的关系	I have a special relationship with my aunt.
她是我们的邻居	She is our neighbor
女人并不总是女士	Women are not always ladies
你的妻子是意大利人	Your wife is Italian
什么是革命？	What is a revolution?
我有女朋友	I have a girlfriend
她是一个人	She is a person

这是我的文化	This is my culture
我们是好人	We are good people
他去了工会	He went to the union
人性是独一无二的	Humanity is unique

训练时间

农民	Farmer
公民	Citizen
我的队友	My teammate
男孩们在体育场训练	The boys train in the stadium
她没有敌人	She has no enemies
孩子喝葡萄汁	The child drinks grape juice
谁是青少年？	Who is a teenager?
这位女士负责	This lady is responsible
她是一个有品格的女人	She is a woman with character
观众听到了	The audience heard
你姐姐是我的新娘	Your sister is my bride
人类吃肉	Humans eat meat
人群听取了国王的意见	The crowd listened to the views of the king
你有很好的习俗	You have good customs
什么时候举行婚礼？	When is the wedding?
什么是公民？	What is a citizen?
客人也工作	Guests also work
吉尔伯托是一个人	Gilberto is a person
人们看	People watch
你没有文化	You have no culture
他们是好人	They are good people
狗是人类最好的朋友	The dog is man's best friend

我们是一对吗？	Are we a pair?
他不知道他的年龄	He doesn't know his age
多么美好的习惯	What a good habit

训练时间

该小组访问了医院	The team visited the hospital
他们是新邻居	They are new neighbors
革命现在开始了！	The revolution is now beginning!
他是我工作的同事	He is a colleague of my work.
他是我的邻居之一	He is one of my neighbors
我们很努力	We work hard
猫是一种很好的动物	The cat is a very good animal
我的叔叔写了关于旅游的文章	My uncle wrote an article about travel.
老人很重要	The elderly are very important
不，他不是我的男朋友	No, he is not my boyfriend.
她是一个非常有趣的人	She is a very interesting person
对一般人群而言	For the general population
他是我的室友	He is my roommate
他们是小成年人	They are small adults
你是受害者吗？	Are you a victim?
这是个人	This is an individual
你已经是成年人了	You are already an adult
她看着女孩们	She looks at the girls

这对人类不利	This is not good for humans
我也不是	Neither do I
你有敌人吗？	Do you have an enemy?
他们研究旅游业	They study tourism
他们是军官	They are officers
我有一个敌人	I have an enemy

训练时间

我们有一个协会	We have an association
此外，我们没有证人	In addition, we have no witnesses
他永远是个绅士	He will always be a gentleman
我表兄弟去参加博览会	My cousin went to the fair.
我不想要葡萄酒，但我想喝水	I don't want wine, but I want to drink water.
我是一名目击者	I am an eyewitness
青年为什么不学习？	Why don't young people learn?
这不是一个好婚姻	This is not a good marriage
我不为我的朋友买单	I don't pay for my friend.
我们是这里的受害者	We are the victims here
我的伴侣允许它	My partner allowed it
医生明天会收到结果	The doctor will receive the results tomorrow
老师给我们读了一本书	The teacher read a book for us.

他很好地对待他的员工	He treats his staff very well
我们有三个不同的地方	We have three different places
我父亲非常爱她	My father loves her very much.
公民社会非常重要	Civil society is very important

训练时间

故事模式

ENGLISH

Reporter: "There are so many people at this year's carnival. I have seen my neighbor and a colleague with a flag. Let me go to the peasant area and talk to some people there."

"Hello everyone, welcome to the 24th Green Carnival, how are you today?"

Visitor 1: "We are doing very well, we are enjoying this exhibition."

Reporter: "I am very happy to know that I can ask you about your clothing? What is the theme?"

Visitor 1: "We are Portuguese citizens, a country with a population of 11 million, and we have a unique culture. In answering your second question, our theme this year is "humanity tourism."

Visitor 2: "We have all witnessed the destructive power of the hurricane, so we decided to help raise awareness and make donations for the victims."

CHINESE

记者: "在今年的狂欢节上有这么多人。我见过我的邻居和一位带旗帜的同事。让我去农民区与那里的一些人交谈。"

"**大家好**,欢迎参加第24届绿色嘉年华,今天你好吗?"

访客1: "**我们**做得很好,我们很享受这个展览。"

记者: "**我很高兴**知道我可以问你关于你的服装吗?主题是什么?"

访客1: "**我们**是葡萄牙公民,人口1100**万的国家**,**我们**有独特的文化。在回答第二个问题时,我们今年的主题是 **人**类旅游。"

访客2: "**我们**都目睹了飓风的破坏力,所以我们决定帮助提高认识并为受害者捐款。"

第21章

编号

关键词：Number, one, two, three, four, five, six, seven, eight, nine, ten, eleven, twelve, thirteen, fourteen, fifteen, sixty, seventy, one thousand, one million, twenty.

一	One
二	Two
三	Three
四	Four
五	Five
六	Six
七	Seven
八	Eight
九	Nine
十	Ten
十一	Eleven
十二	Twelve
十三	Thirteen
十四	Fourteen
十五	Fifteen
两个和四个是六个	Two and four are six
两个和六个是八个	Two and six are eight
五个女人	Five women
他们看到六头大象	They saw six elephants
四个苹果	Four apples
第五页	Fifth page
我们有八页	We have eight pages
我有四块钱	I have four dollars.
五个苹果	Five apples
我有两个姐妹	I have two sisters.

训练时间

二十	Twenty
三十	Thirty
四十	Forty
谁是头号人物？	Who is the number one?
三是素数	The third is the prime number
他的阿姨有三只猫	His aunt has three cats
她是我的第三个女朋友	She is my third girlfriend
我等一下	I will wait.
他是她的第一个孩子	He is her first child
车站距离这里2米	The station is 2 meters away from here.
你不想要第二碗米饭	You don't want the second bowl of rice
他的第一件粉色衬衫	His first pink shirt
他是七个孩子中的第六个	He is the sixth of seven children
食谱适合六个人	Recipes for six people
他六点钟来到这里，而不是之前	He came here at six o'clock instead of before
第四盘面食适合他	The fourth dish is suitable for him.
四个男朋友吃什么？	What do four boyfriends eat?
非常感谢！	Thank you very much!
五十或四十？	Fifty or forty?
我有十八匹马	I have eighteen horses.
从零到十	From zero to ten

他是这个家庭中的第九个男孩	He is the ninth boy in this family.
我儿子十岁了	My son is ten years old.
我们是十一个人	We are eleven people
他有十二个儿子	He has twelve sons

训练时间

半	Half
米	Meter
我有一些钱	I have some money
他有八个孙子。	He has eight grandchildren.
我有十三只猫	I have thirteen cats
十四个表兄弟	Fourteen cousins
我十五岁	I was fifteen years old
接下来的十二个小时	The next twelve hours
你为什么不来过我们的六岁生日？	Why didn't you come to our sixth birthday?
有五个人的桌子吗？	Is there a table for five people?
我们总共八个	We have a total of eight
我们到达第十名	We reached the tenth place
十分钟	Ten minutes
数量很高	High quantity
他只有十七岁	He is only seventeen years old
我从八到十一学习	I am studying from eight to eleven
我下午三点左右喝茶	I drink tea around three in the afternoon.
十二年，一只狗老了	Twelve years old, a dog is old
我有十四件白衬衫	I have fourteen white shirts.

我十一点睡觉了	I slept at eleven o'clock.
我们有二十匹马	We have twenty horses
他们吃了一些苹果	They ate some apples
六分之一是三	One sixth is three
现在是十点半	It's half past ten
第五座桥通向博物馆	The fifth bridge leads to the museum

训练时间

万	Million
四个人	Four people
一双鞋	A pair of shoes
七十一个胡萝卜	Seventy-one carrots
这是一百万美元	This is one million dollars
我姑姑大概四十岁了	My aunt is about forty years old.
我是八十年代的	I am in the 1980s.
我读了九十分钟	I read for 90 minutes.
蛋糕在烤箱中保持60分钟	The cake is kept in the oven for 60 minutes
一米	One meter
第三	Third
今天是第三天	Today is the third day
这是你的一半	This is half of you
目前，他排名第八	Currently, he is ranked eighth
我们已经等了大约六十年了	We have been waiting for about sixty years.
我差不多七十岁了	I am almost seventy years old.
七十个男人吃鸡肉	Seventy men eat chicken
他记得七十年代	He remembers the seventies

下周是我的最后一周	Next week is my last week.
我没有任何答案	I don't have any answers.
博物馆九点开放	The museum is open at nine
他们要求至少一百万	They demand at least one million
五米	Five meters
数千公里	Thousands of kilometers
七是她的号码	Seven is her number

训练时间

其中一百个非常好	One hundred of them are very good
五位老师	Five teachers
你有一千个朋友	You have a thousand friends
他是我年龄的两倍	He is twice my age
这里有很多人	There are many people here.
你比他大多少？	How much are you bigger than him?
我叔叔的车比较小	My uncle's car is small
十减四等于六	Ten minus four equals six
他的兄弟不到五个	His brother is less than five
我们有足够的时间	We have enough time
她买几件衣服	She bought a few clothes
为什么许多人死亡？	Why do many people die?
我们吃了一半的面包	We ate half of the bread
他吃了很多鱼	He ate a lot of fish

他的鞋子是蓝色的	His shoes are blue
我九点吃晚饭	I have dinner at nine.
现在她已经十八岁了	Now she is eighteen years old.
你有更大的东西吗？	Do you have something bigger?
一周的第七天是星期六	The seventh day of the week is Saturday
这个月的第五个星期天	The fifth Sunday of the month
五辆白色轿车	Five white cars
厨师有四十公斤肉	The chef has forty kilograms of meat
她第九次去超市	Her ninth trip to the supermarket
三十年后我们在同一个城市	Thirty years later we are in the same city
二十个家庭住在这里	Twenty families live here
来自亚洲的三十六种橙子	Thirty-six kinds of oranges from Asia
玛丽亚有四十四只企鹅	Maria has forty-four penguins
来自意大利的35人	35 people from Italy
汉有四十三只动物	Han has forty-three animals
这个男人已经六十岁了	This man is sixty years old.
我女朋友十九岁	My girlfriend is 19 years old
今晚，他排名第七	Tonight, he is ranked seventh.
我下午一点喝咖啡	I have a little coffee in the afternoon.
我的儿子十六岁	My son is sixteen
她有两千本书	She has two thousand books

这是一双好鞋

这个城市有200万人口

This is a good pair of shoes

The city has a population of 2 million

训练时间

故事模式

ENGLISH

"Can you remember what we learned yesterday, Xu?" said Huang.
"If you can, half of my work will end. If you can't, you should work harder if you want to pass the exam."
"Yes, I can." Xu said.
"Great! Let's continue."
"Two plus two is four, three plus one is four, one plus three equals four, eight divided by two equals four."
"Very good, let us pay more attention to them now, starting with the sixth. Can you tell me about the sixth?" Huang said.

"Six plus one equals seven, six plus three equals nine, six plus four equals ten, seven plus six equals thirteen, six plus six equals twelve, six plus four equals ten."

"Good job Xu. Now answer these questions. If I have 14 fans on Snapchat, and you have fifteen, what is the sum of these two fans?"

"Twenty-nine fans," Xu replied.

CHINESE

"你能记得昨天我们学到了什么,徐?"黄说。

"如果可以的话,我的一半工作将会结束。如果你不能,你应该**努力工作**,如果你想**通**过考试。"

"是的,我可以,"徐说。

"好极了!让我们继续吧。"

"两加二是四,三加一是四,一加三等于四,八除二等于四"

"非常好,让我们现在更加关注他们,从第六位开始。你能告诉我第六次吗?"黄说。

"六加一等于七,六加三等于九,六加四等于十,七加六等于十三,六加六等于十二,六加四等于十。"

"好徐。 现在来回答这些问题。 如果我在Snapchat上有14个粉丝,而你有15个,这两个粉丝的总和是多少?"

"二十九个粉丝,"徐回答道。

10 20 30 40 50 60 70 80 90 100

书的结尾一

要获得完整的体验,请获取该系列中的其他书籍

学习英语的简单方法

对于下一本书的更新,或者如果你只是想讨论这个,你可以在twitter和facebook上使用@badcreativ3
www.facebook.com/BadCreativ3

其他BADCREATIVE书

The Simplest Way To Learn French

The Simplest Way To Learn Spanish

The Simplest Way To Learn Portuguese

感谢您购买,不要忘记在我们的亚马逊页面上给我们评论。

www.ingramcontent.com/pod-product-compliance
Lightning Source LLC
Chambersburg PA
CBHW072013110526
44592CB00012B/1283